Machine Learning:

2 manuscript: Machine Learning for Beginners, Machine Learning with Python

By Daniel Géron

By reading this document, the reader agrees that under no circumstances is the author responsible for any losses, direct or indirect, which are incurred as a result of the use of information contained within this document, including, but not limited to, — errors, omissions, or inaccuracies.

4

5

Machine Learning for Beginners:

Step-by-Step Guide to Learning and Mastering Machine Learning for Absolute Beginners with Real Examples

Introduction

Congratulations for purchasing Machine Learning for absolute beginners: step-by-step guide to learning and mastering machine learning for absolute beginners.

The object of this book is providing an in-depth comprehension of machine learning methods to absolute beginners. This book explains the basics and fundamentals of machine learning that will help acquire and develop basic understanding of machine learning technics.

Machine learning is used nowadays in different fields in our era. This book will help to understand the concepts of machine learning, the different types of machine learning as well as when they are applied. This book has four main chapters. The first chapter presents the big picture of the concepts of machine learning. The second chapter provide a presentation of the different types of machines learning paradigms. The third chapter give an in-depth explanation of artificial neural networks. The fourth chapter give a presentation of the different algorithms used to train machine learning models as well as artificial neural networks.

In the first chapter of this book, we provide an introduction of machine learning concept. We explain the philosophy behind machine learning. We also explain when machine learning can be applied and when it is better to use other alternative. We present the advantages and the challenges of implementing a machine learning model to solve a specific problem. We also list some examples of machine learning applications in this chapter. Finally, we present briefly how a machine learning model can be implemented.

In chapter two, we go through the different types of machine learning namely Supervised learning, unsupervised learning, semi-supervised learning and reinforcement learning. For each type of machine learning we explain for which application it can be used. We also explain the advantages and the challenges of each type.

Chapter three of this book provide the details of artificial neural networks. It explains first the fundamentals and the concept of artificial neural networks. It also presents the different components of an artificial neural network which include neurons and activation functions. In this chapter we explain how neurons works. We also present the different activation functions that can be used in artificial neural networks and we provide the difference between these activation functions as well as when each activation function is best used.

In this chapter we go through the different major types of artificial neural networks as well as the when each type is used. We explain in this chapter how to develop an artificial neural network. We also present the general rules that should be considered in developing an artificial neural network, the loss functions that can be used. We explain as well how we should split and use the data to train an artificial neural network as well as the concepts behind feed forward and back propagation to train artificial neural networks. Finally, we explain briefly the procedure to train an artificial neural network.

Chapter four of this book, tackles the learning algorithm. We present the gradient descent algorithm as well the variants of the gradient descent algorithm namely the stochastic, batch and mini-batch gradient descent algorithms. We also present the Adam algorithm, a recent optimization algorithm developed specifically for training artificial neural networks.

Machine learning is a powerful tool to convert data into valuable information that serves a particular purpose. In this book, we will learn how to use this tool to develop powerful models and different technics that can be used.

There are plenty of books on this subject on the market, thanks again for choosing this one! Every effort was made to ensure it is full of as much useful information as possible, please enjoy!

Chapter 1: Basics of machine learning

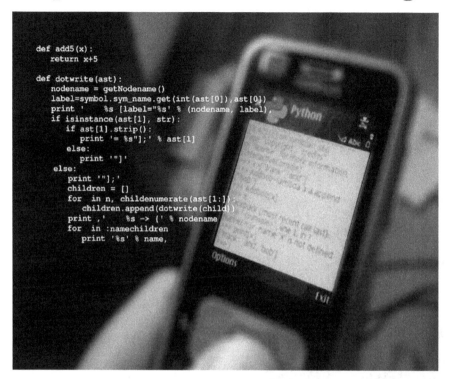

Nowadays machine learning is used and influence every aspect of our lives. Marketing, health care, social media, banking systems, stock market and many other systems use machine learning to target clients, provide customized products, to filter and detect disease, anomaly, fraudulent transactions as well as to grow and improve business. Machine learning relies on the concept of developing cost-effective programs that learns from the data in order to identify trends and make optimal decisions with minimum human intervention. The powerful computer systems and the digitalized data available in this era made machine learning a powerful tool to solve complex problems efficiently at a low cost.

In this chapter, we will first go into an in-depth explanation of machine learning concept. We will define cases when to use machine learning and cases when other simpler deterministic approaches are the go-to approach to solve the problem in hand. Finally, we will explain the advantages of machine learning and provide examples of problems that can be solved by machine learning. Let's first start with understanding what machine learning is.

1.1 *What is machine learning?*

```
<!DOCTYPE html PUBLIC "-//W3C//DTD
<html dir="ltr" xmlns="http://www.
<head>
    <title>Hello World</title>
    <meta http-equiv="Content-Type
    <meta name="keywords" content
    <meta name="description" con
    <meta name="content-language
    <link rel="stylesheet" type
</head>
body>
<div class="banner">
<div style="margin:0 au
```

Machine learning is whole complete branch of Artificial Intelligence and computer science. The later is an emerging science to build machine programs that are able to mimic the human behavior and take decisions efficiently like a human would do. Artificial intelligence relies on several algorithms to build these intelligent systems that requires no human guidance to make predictions and decisions.

The idea is, instead of developing algorithms with imposed rules to perform a specific task, we develop algorithms that learn from themselves to perform this task. These algorithms are what we call machine learning. The role of machine learning algorithms is to acquire knowledge and learn as much as possible from data in order to identify trends, make future predictions or decisions based on the learned knowledge. Machine learning combine statistical methods and the power of computers to detect hidden patterns and behaviors in order to perform predictions.

For instance, machine learning proposes recommendations of news, videos, movies, etc. on YouTube, Netflix, websites based on the information gathered about you when you consulted these websites. These platforms collect the maximum of data about you to learn your behaviors. Then it predicts what you might like and provide recommendations based on that. Cloud computing and the increasing storage capacity of machines as well as the personalized chips have served and gave the major breakthrough of machine learning advancements.

Machine learning are data driven programs in the sense that they rely solely on data to make predictions and decisions. They learn and acquire knowledge only from data and improve their performance with more data. They rely on probabilities rather than logic to map the hidden patterns in data. Machine learning works mainly as a black box that takes as input a set of data, processes it and produce an outcome. We refer to machine learning as a black box because we don't understand the details of the relationship that relates the outcome produced by the machine learning to the input data. Machine learning tries to emulate in some way how the human brain works.

For example, when we play a game, we make a guess about the most likely action to make in order to win the game. When driving somewhere, we try to find the best and fastest route to reach our desired destination. When making a trade, we try to make the best trade with the least risk and high income generating. All these example tasks are done based on the human intelligence with unconsciously made decisions. Instead of analyzing and reasoning, the brain unconsciously tries to estimate how likely something can happen. For instance, the stock is a high volatile market where logic and reasoning might not be the choice to make decision but probabilities based on passed experiences might be a more successful strategy.

On the same concept, machine learning makes decisions and predictions on how likely something can happen based on past experiences. These experiences are reflected by the collected datasets. Machine learning is very powerful at predicting how likely something might happen or to be in a specific state because machines are very efficient to compute probabilities.

Because of the emerging powerful machines and computers that are to make fast calculations, another type of learning has been develop which is deep learning. Deep learning is a domain of machine learning that consist of breaking a problem into several chunks of sub-problems to be treated separately. The deep learning is mainly based on artificial neural networks.

 The neural networks were developed to mimic the connections and functioning of the neurons in the human brain. When artificial neural networks are fed with data or information, they break the information into chunks where each chunk is processed by a neuron. Then these neurons are connected to each other to communicate the information in order to produce a targeted outcome. For example, we a person look at an image of an animal, the human brain process information like color, size, shape among others to make a guess about the animal in the picture. In the same way, artificial neural networks break the same information based on the pixels of the image to recognize the animal in the picture.

Machine learning algorithms are powerful tools as long as the data are accurate. In fact, as mentioned before machine learning are a data-driven programs. They rely on data to make predictions. In order to develop a fully working and performant machine learning model ready to make predictions and decisions, this model should be trained and fitted on data.

In other words, we should train the model on the input data and the expected outcome first. This is usually done with an optimization algorithm the minimize the error of the predicted value by the model. We will go into the details of the process to build a machine learning model later in this chapter. Now that we understand the concept behind machine learning, let's learn when machine learning is the go-to method to solve or problem and when to avoid it.

1.2   *When to use and when to avoid machine learning?*

In order to make the best outcome and fully take advantage of machine learning, it is very important to understand when to use machine learning and when it is best to avoid machine learning. Indeed, some problems are best solved with a simple deterministic rule-based approach.

A rule-based approach is a system that consist of an ensemble of rules that are imposed based on the knowledge or the expertise of user. These rules are imposed to perform a specific task. These systems are also called expert systems because they rely mainly on the expertise of the user. These systems are based on rules developed using logic and reasoning to perform a task unlike machine learning that are based on probabilities to perform the same task.

Let's consider for example a person applies for a loan from a bank. A rule-based system would for example, set a rule if a person has an income under $1000, the requested loan is denied. Therefore, this person would be accorded the loan only if it has an income over $1000. A machine learning program would use other information about this person, estimate how likely this person is able to refund the loan then make a decision whether to accord or deny the loan to this person.

Machine learning is a data-driven approach. Hence it implies availability of large datasets in order to make accurate decisions. In case only a limited dataset is available to solve a particular problem, it is best to use a deterministic approach. When limited dataset is available it is hard to train a machine learning model and generalize its applicability to other similar problem. The developed model in this case is only applicable for the few data it was trained on.

Because machine learning methods rely solely only on data and the human expertise or judgment is not taken in consideration, it is the data that dictate if the machine learning method will fail or succeed to perform the task it was designed for. The way a machine learning approach works is that a modeler develops a learning algorithm. Then the modeler feed the learning algorithm with the data and information.

The algorithm learns by itself from the data with no guidance or human interference. It is the algorithm that builds the system. If the data provided for the algorithm is of poor quality and biased then the system is also of poor quality and biased. Hence, cleaning and acquiring the right data to solve a problem with machine learning problem is very crucial. If the data are biases and noisy it is better to stick with a traditional method. Otherwise the machine learning method will memorize the noise and provide inaccurate results.

Because they are developed to process large dataset, machine learning methods require significant time and computation resources and storage capacity. If these resources are limited then a deterministic method might be a better approach to adopt.

Machine learning methods comes handy in three scenarios: 1)when the human expertise is very limited to solve a complex problem, 2) when it is difficult to transform the human expertise into a program, 3) or when it time consuming to setup up procedure to solve a simple problem although the human expertise and the possibility of implementing that expertise into a program.

Let's the example of filtering emails into Inbox, spams, and ad. A human can easily filter an email as spam or ad. However, it would very tedious to do the same task for large number of emails. A machine learning algorithm can do the same task more efficiently.

1.3   *Advantages and challenges of using machine learning*

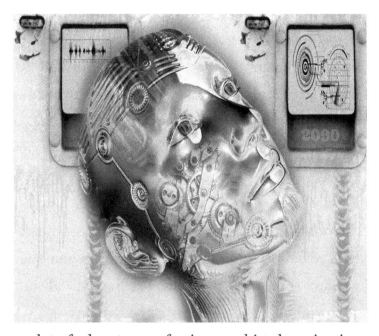

There are lot of advantages of using machine learning in cases it is suited to use a machine learning approach. First of all, machine learning programs are able to convert data into valuable information. That is the core idea behind machine learning which is making data reveal hidden information and patterns to improve our understanding of different phenomena whether it is for financial improvement and increase profit or for medical and human understanding.

Machine learning programs are able to easily identify trend and hidden patterns in large datasets that would be tedious for human beings to detect. Another advantage of machine learning is no human intervention or expertise is needed to learn from the data. Machine learning programs are continuously improving their accuracy and gaining experience with the increasing of data quantity. As long as data is growing and fed to the machine learning algorithms, they keep improving their performance and making more accurate predictions and decisions.

The major advantage of machine learning is that they are able of handling multi-variable and multi-dimensional dataset. Although its advantages and their efficiency, machine learning algorithms have some disadvantages. The main disadvantage is the need to acquire large dataset with good quality and unbiased. Implementing a machine learning approach has some challenges which are the ability to interpret the results and to detect the susceptible errors.

Indeed, machine learning methods are able to extract valuable information from data. But without appropriate interpretation that valuable information is not useful. Also, without the ability to detect susceptible errors that might be caused by plausible data bias, that information provided by the machine learning algorithm might be misleading and would yield to biased results.

Overall, the main challenge to implement a machine learning algorithm is acquiring good quality data and having the capacity to analyze the data and interpret the results together with the ability to point towards the plausible source of errors. Another direct challenge of implementing a machine learning algorithm is the ability to convert raw data into formatted usable data that can be processed machine learning algorithms.

1.4   *Examples of machine learning problems*

Machine learning nowadays is the major advancement technology worldwide. It is present in lot of fields. The availability of large quantities of data, the increasing performance of computers are the reason for the dominance of machine learning in every field. In this sub-section we will talk about few fields where machine learning is used.

Machine learning is very handy for data security and anomaly detection in systems. For instance, in a cloud system machine learning algorithm identify patterns on ways of gaining access to the cloud to flag anomalies that could be security flaws. In the same category fraud detection and suspicious transactions in general are better detected with machine learning algorithms.

Stock market and financial trading now benefit from the power of machine learning. The reason for that is machines are very efficient in computing probabilities and processing the huge quantities of data at a high speed. The stock market is high volatile stochastic market where trades are made on high scale of speed and volume. Humans cannot compete with machines at this level. Many firms nowadays rely on machines to make predictions and perform trades.

Healthcare is another field that now uses machine learning methods. They are mainly used to analyze scans and MRIs to detect diseases. They are also used to learn the causes or risk factors that lead to a certain disease.

Marketing and e-commerce are fields that benefit the most from machine learning methods to target clients and improve profits. More precisely customized marketing is a field that relies basically on machine learning. It is based on the concept of the more you know your clients and their behaviors the better you can provide them customized services.

Hence, the more you sell and increase profit. These systems gather information from the clients according to the website they visit and the products they have seen without buying or they bought. Then, the system will generate e-mails or ads and/or coupons of the product they checked without buying or similar products.

Using the same concept as customized marketing, recommendations on Netflix, YouTube, Facebook, Amazon among others, are based on machine learning algorithms. The algorithms analyze your behaviors and activities to make a guess about what you might like to buy or watch.

These systems get smarter and efficient with the more data they can gather. Speech and image recognition as well as natural language processing are also a widely application of machine learning algorithms.

Now that you understand the philosophy behind machine learning and potential applications of machine learning as well as the challenges to implement it, let's go through the major steps to develop a machine learning model to solve any problem.

1.5 *How to develop a machine learning model?*

Before starting any modelling, it is essential to fix beforehand the objectives and the outcome of implementing a machine learning model. At this step, you should set the goals on the key problem that would be solved and the questions that you are trying to answer by the machine learning model. First, you should set hypotheses regarding the problem you have in hand as well as some potential strategies to solve it and plausible inputs to feed the model.

Developing a machine learning model becomes then an iterative process that involves going through the cycle of setting a hypothesis, testing/training and validating. Collecting and gathering data is a crucial step in developing a machine learning model. This step not only implies identifying and collecting the required data to test a hypothesis but also cleaning and formatting these data into usable format. At this phase, you

28

should make sure the data are unbiased and does not include outliers that may impact the results produced by the model.

Analyzing and visualizing these data help detect bias and verify the quality of the data. After the collection and the preparation of data you can build a model and test it against a set of data then validate it against new data. The testing process implies training the model and adjusting parameters that impact the model accuracy. Validation of the model helps assessing the model accuracy based on performance metrics.

At this stage, you assess whether the model produces the expected results and answer to the questions you fixed at the beginning. You can iterate the process by testing different hypothesis or models until you reach satisfactory results and the desired outcome.

In the next chapters of the book, we will learn the different types of machine learning that can be used and when they applicable. We will also expand over how to develop a machine learning model and presenting the tools to test and validate a machine learning model.

Chapter 2: Machine learning types

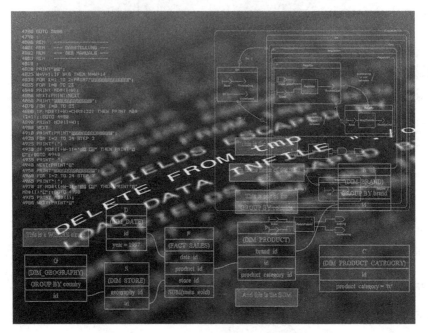

The are different types of machine learning models that can be classed into four categories: supervised, unsupervised, semi-supervised and reinforcement learning.

2.1 *Supervised Learning*

Supervised learning is a machine learning paradigm with a goal of estimating a relationship between inputs and outputs. This function is called the mapping function. The mapping function describes the hidden patterns in the data. In supervised learning we typically have a labeled dataset that consist of pairs of input data (usually a vector) and a target output.

The target output is a value associated with the input data. The supervised learning algorithm process the training labeled dataset in order to estimates a mapping function that is used to estimate or predict similar new datasets. In other words, the learning algorithm is generalized into new unseen examples with acceptable accuracy.

Let's consider a vector $\mathbf{X}$ of input data and $\mathbf{Y}$ is the target output value. Formally, the supervised learning algorithm tries to estimates the mapping function f such as $f(\mathbf{X}) = \mathbf{Y}$. Realistically, we are looking for f such that $\mathbf{Y} = f(\mathbf{X}) + \varepsilon$ with ε is an error which is random with a mean zero. We want ε to be as small as possible.

Two main tasks can be performed with supervised learning which are *classification* and *regression*. Classification is mainly done when the output data are a discrete variable. A discrete variable can be a quality or category data for example men or women, smoker or non-smoker. In contrast, regression is mainly used when the output variable is a continuous variable (i.e. quantity variable) like price of a house, number clients, age.

A linear regression model is the simplest approach to model a regression problem. Regarding classification, a number of different approaches can be considered like logistic regression, decision tree, random forest or multilayer perceptron.

The later is a type of artificial neural networks that will be covered in next chapter of this book. In this section we will cover the basic algorithms that are used for classification and regression which are **logistic** and **linear** regression.

Logistic regression

Logistic regression has the goal of classifying discrete variables or binary variables (i.e. 0 or 1 /yes or no). Given a set of input data **X,** we are looking for a function f that estimates the target value **Y** such that $Y = f(X)$. In a logistic problem f is the logistic function or what is called the sigmoid function. The logistic function is given by the following equation: $F(X) = L / (1 + exp(-X))$. This function is based on probabilities. The sigmoid function is a logistic function with L equal to 1. This function has values between 0 and 1. The sigmoid or logistic function transforms any value into ranges between 0 and 1. This is a desired characteristic in machine learning to estimates probabilities of an input to belong to a specific class.

The logistic regression requires a transformation of inputs X in order to get values between 0 and 1. The transformation is as follows: $Z = B_0 + B_1 * X$. The regression is then performed using the new variable Z. To develop a logistic regression model, we need an objective function or what is called loss or cost function.

The loss or cost function provides a metric to evaluate the performance and accuracy of the model. In a logistic regression problem this function is given as follows according to the target value:

Loss function = $- \log \{1/ [1 + exp(-Z)]\}$ if the target value y is equal to 1

Loss function = $- \log \{1- 1/ [1 + exp(-Z)]\}$ if the target value y is equal to 0

These two equations can be merged into one single equation as given below:

Loss function = - (1 /n) * $\sum$ [y * log (h(Z)) + (1 - y) * log (1 – h (Z))]

with h is the sigmoid function given by the equation: h(X) = 1/ (1 + exp (-X).

Linear regression

Linear regression aims at providing a linear relationship between inputs and quantity outputs. The mapping function of a linear regression is as linear function. Given a set of input data **X,** we are looking for a function f that estimates the target value **Y:** **Y** = f (**X**) = W * **X** + B, with W and B are the parameters to the model. The parameter W is called the weight and B is called intercept or bias. Training a model is the process of estimating the parameters W and B. As for the logistic regression, we need a lost or cost function that provides a metric of the model accuracy. In linear regression model, the cost function a function that quantifies the distance between the actual value of the output and the estimated value by the model.
Mathematically, the cost function is:

Loss function = $(1/m) * \sum (y_{predicted} - y_{target})^2$, with $y_{predicted}$ and y_{target} are the predicted and true output value resp. In this case, the loss function is nothing else than the Root Mean Squared Error (RMSE) between the mode output and the actual value.

The parameters W and B are estimates such that the loss function is small as possible. In order to do so, we use an optimization algorithm. There are different optimization algorithms available. We will cover the optimization algorithms in Chapter 4.

2.2 _Unsupervised learning_

Unsupervised learning is mainly used when the data is unlabeled. In other words, the input data are available but the outcome of this data is completely unknown. Unlike the supervised learning, there is no correct or training dataset to learn from. In this case, the machine learning algorithm or specifically the unsupervised learning algorithm is designed to learn from the data itself without additional information or guidance to constrain the output.

The unsupervised learning algorithms are based on similarities, differences and patterns to learn the hidden structure in the data. The unsupervised learning can be used for **clustering**, **association** and **anomaly detection**.

Clustering aims at identifying the inherent groupings in data. Association has the goal to detect and describe patterns that happen together in a dataset. Finally, anomaly detection aims at detecting unusual data points within a dataset.

Clustering

Clustering is mainly applied for grouping data into groups or what's commonly called clusters. A cluster is a set of data sharing similar characteristics. Clustering is important to determine the inherent grouping in unlabeled datasets. There is no guidance on how to cluster data and depends on the needs of the user.

The data can be classified as to define homogenous groups in data or typical data. In contract, the data can be classified unusual a-typical data or outliers. Finding the homogenous and typical data can be useful for space reduction and describing patterns for dominant data or clusters. In the other hand, finding the outliers or atypical data can be very useful to understand the unusual patterns.

Clustering is very handy in different domains such as marketing or targeted marketing to groups clients for customized marketing, biology to classify different species in order to better study them, planning to group houses and analyze their risk of inundation based on their location, insurance and banking to classify customers as well as their policies, transactions and detect fraudulent transactions.

Usually, the clustering algorithms use a similarity measure to identify clusters in the data. The similarity measure can be defined as Euclidean distance or a probabilistic distance. Several algorithms can be used for clustering. These algorithms can be classified as density, hierarchical, partitioning or grid-based methods. The density-based methods consist of classifying data based on their density in the data space. Every dense region is considered as a cluster with similarities and different from the other lower dense region.

 Hierarchical clustering forms clusters based on pre-defined clusters. The algorithm starts with all data in the same clusters and divide it into several clusters or starts with each data point as single cluster and merge them into clusters iteratively. Partitioning based methods on the other hand, split data into k clusters such that it optimizes a criterion reflecting the similarity between groups within each cluster. Finally, the grid-based methods discretize the data space into a grid structure and the clustering is performed on the grid. In this book we will cover the widely used algorithms of each category. We start first the most popular algorithm the k-means algorithm

The k-means algorithm belongs the partitioning category of clustering algorithms. It is an algorithm the is based on centroids meaning that the data points are classified according to their distance into the centroid of a cluster. Centroid is the center of a cluster. The algorithm starts with a random k clusters formed randomly from the data. Every point of the data is assigned to a cluster such that the distance between the point and the cluster centroid is small.

Then, for each cluster the centroids are recalculated. The algorithm repeats this procedure iteratively until it reaches a convergence criterion. This criterion can be a non-significant change in data forming clusters meaning the centroid is similar or a maximum of number of iterations is attained or a non-significant change in the re-assignment of data to clusters. Note that the number of clusters k is a user-defined parameter that should be fixed beforehand. This algorithm is widely used because it is very straightforward to implement it, simple to understand and computationally efficient. However, this algorithm suffers from some drawbacks.

This algorithm is only applicable when data are continuous and the mean is defined. Indeed, the cluster centroid is defined based on the mean of data. If the mean is not defined for the data other functions should be used to define the centroid. For instance, if the data are categorial or binary, the centroid can be defined based on the k-mode. The k-mode provides the frequency of values. This algorithm is also sensitive to outliers in data because it is based on the mean which is not a robust statistic.

The mean is highly sensitive and can easily change significantly when an outlier exists in data. Another downside of this algorithm is the fact that is a deterministic algorithm in the sense that each point is assigned to one cluster and a cluster only. However, in reality data points might fit in different clusters and clusters may be overlapping. The k-means algorithm, the way it defines clusters, cannot define overlapping clusters.

Gaussian mixture models are a distribution base method that help overcoming some issues mentioned for k-means algorithm. The gaussian mixture models uses mean, covariance and the size or weight or define each cluster. As mentioned, this type of algorithms uses the distribution of data to define the clusters within a dataset.

Self-organizing maps is a grid-based method that is fully defined as an artificial neural network. This category of artificial neural network is different than artificial neural network typically used and covered in the next chapter of this book. The self-organizing maps has the goal of discretizing the data space. It uses a competitive leaning and a neighborhood function to preserve the data shape that is fed to the model.

Association

Association has the of describing patterns and data features that happens frequently together and are correlated. For instance, patient that have diabetes might have high blood pressure. In contrast with clustering, association help identify the data features that happen together and maps the relationship between the features. Clustering help identify data points that are related and have similar features.

For instance, if we represent the data as a table where each row is a data point with features given in each column, clustering classifies the rows together (i.e. data points) while association find hidden relationship between the columns (i.e. features). Association is very handy in different domains. In marketing, association will provide information about the products that are usually both together. Given this information, the products will be put in the same aisle in the store. Association has different applications in health care. For example, analyzing eating habits in patients with a certain disease which might help understand whether certain foods might cause it, or used to understand the diseases that have high probability of occurring together. The association cane be sued in genetics science to have a better understanding of which genes are trigged together. It can be applied in city planning to detect busy traffic intersections. So now how do the association rule work?

Association identify the co-occurrence of data features. It helps answer the question if A happens what is the other feature B that is highly probable to occur. In short, association rule detects the hidden if-then associations in large datasets. These if-then associations are what is commonly named as association rules in machine learning. The two parts of the association rule are called the *antecedent* for the if part (i.e. A) and *consequent* for the then part (i.e. B).

Association relies on three metrics to identify the associations rules namely *support, confidence* and *lift*. Support and confidence are metrics used to measure how powerful the relationship between two features or the rule (if A then B). Lift is a metric to measure the level of confidence to assign to the rule by comparing the confidence of the rule with an anticipated confidence.

Support is defined as the number of times A and B occur together. In other words, support is the frequency of the A and B occurring together which can be estimated as the fraction of events of A and B occurring together. Support provides the marginal probability p (A). Confidence, in the other hand, measures how many times B occurred when A occurred.

In other words, how many times B occur when A occur. Confidence provides then the conditional probability of B knowing that A occurred which is p (B/A). Overall, support answer the question how frequent is the rule if A then B. If it has high frequency then it is worth considering the rule. Confidence answer the question how many times the rule if A then B is true. The lift is the ratio of confidence and support. If the lift value is above 1 than A and B are positively correlated, if it is less than 1 then they are negatively correlated. If the lift is 1 than A and B are not correlated. In order to use an association rule learning algorithm a minimum threshold support value and a minimum threshold confidence value should be imposed to the algorithm.

The algorithm then provides all association rules that have a support value equal or above the minimum threshold support value and confidence value equal or above the minimum threshold confidence value that were imposed.

There are different algorithms to use for an association rule learning. We cite Apriori, SETM and AIS. In this book we will focus on the widely used algorithm the Apriori. This algorithm consists of finding all the rules that have a support greater or equal to a minimum support threshold. To illustrate the functioning of the Apriori, let's denote S as the minimum support threshold, an association rule (if A then B) as R and the number of iterations as i.

The Apriori algorithm starts by generating all sets of rule R having a size equal to 1. The number of iterations is set to 1. The algorithm downsizes rules R with size i such that the support p (R) is less than S. Then it generates all sets of size $i+1$ such that these sets include the current sets of size i. The algorithm increments the number of iterations ($i = i + 1$) then downsize the rules and so on until it finds all rules with support that is at least the *S* value. Now you are probably thinking but how do algorithm generate sets of rules.

Generation of rules relies on two steps. The first step consists of generating itemset. If we take for example, the association rules for patients with several diseases and we try to understand if a patient have a disease A what is the other disease B that this patient is high likely to get. An itemset in this case would be for instance {diabetes, hypertension, Alzheimer}. The second step is generating rule from each itemset {if diabetes then hypertension and Alzheimer}, {if diabetes and hypertension then Alzheimer} and so on.

So now if we go back to the Apriori algorithm, we said it starts by generating all sets of rules having a size equal to 1. This means in our example it starts by generating itemset where each disease is an itemset such that: {diabetes}, {hypertension}, {Alzheimer}, {dementia}, ... Then from it only keeps the itemset that are frequent among all itemset. At this step only itemset that have a frequency at least the minimum support threshold fixed. In other words, the fraction of cases when this itemset occurred is greater than the minimum threshold.

So, for instance dementia occurs only 5 times in a 1000 times cases which means the fraction is 5/1000 = 0.005. This fraction is very low, then it is not considered as a frequent itemset. The Apriori algorithm relies on the concept of anti-monotone characteristic of support. This concept stipulate that the frequency of subset of an itemset is always greater than the frequency of the itemset itself. To explain this concept let's always consider the patients example.

For instance, if we consider the itemset {diabetes, hypertension}, the frequency of this item set is greater or equal to the frequency of the itemset {diabetes, hypertension, Alzheimer}. Therefore, if an itemset have a support value greater the minimum threshold, all subset of this itemset have a support value greater than the minimum threshold.

We can look at the anti-monotone concept from another angle that is we decrease the size of itemset, we conserve or increase the occurrence frequency of the new itemset. So, the Apriori algorithm after it generates all itemset of size 1 and drops the non-frequent ones, it generates all possible itemset with size equal to 2 formed by the itemset of size 1. Then it keeps only the frequent itemset with size 2 that have support value above the minimum threshold. Then it forms items of size 3 and so on by increasing the size of itemset by 1. After generating frequent itemset, the rules are identified.

The identification of rules consists of generating all possible combination among the items in an itemset. For instance if {diabetes, hypertension, Alzheimer} is our itemset, then the possible rules are : {if diabetes then hypertension, Alzheimer}, {if diabetes and hypertension then Alzheimer}, {if hypertension then diabetes and Alzheimer}, {if hypertension and Alzheimer then diabetes}, {if Alzheimer, then diabetes and hypertension}, {if Alzheimer and diabetes, then hypertension}. Form this possible rules, rules with confidence level that is greater than the minimum confidence threshold are kept.

Confidence has the same property as support which anti-monotone characteristic. As we said explained earlier in this section confidence of a Rule R {if A then B} is the conditional probability of B knowing A.

This means that all subsequent rules generated from the different combination of itemset in Rule R have a confidence lower than the confidence of all items combined.

Let's take an example to better understand the concept. Let's say we have four items A, B, C, D. The confidence of {if A then B, C, D} is lower than the confidence of {if A and B then C and D} which is also lower than {A and B and C then D}. In other words, the rule {A and B and C then D} have the greatest confidence.

This comes from the fact that the support of rules from an itemset is the same. The only difference is towards which itemset the confidence of this rule is calculated. If the number of itemset in the denominator are large than the confidence decrease. Remember the confidence is support (Y) / support (X). If X is formed from few items then it supports is high. Therefore, the confidence of Y will decrease by decreasing items in X. So, the Apriori algorithm downsizes the number of rules following the same procedure as for the frequent elements.

The number of association rules will always depend on the minimum thresholds fixed for the support value and for the confidence value.

Anomaly detection

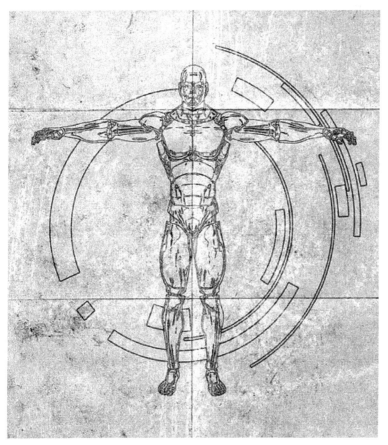

Anomaly detection or outlier detection aims at identifying outliers in a dataset. Before diving into anomaly detection machine learning, let's understand first what are outliers and why they might be important. Outliers are simply data points that are far away from the majority of data points in the space of dataset. Basically, the outliers can be either extreme high values or extreme low values. The outlier data point usually show a different pattern or behavior in the dataset than the rest of the data points. They can be detected visually.

For example, a recorded temperature of 20°C during winter in a Nordic country or a peak flow occurring during winter. In Nordic countries, the peak flow is likely to happen during spring. Depending on the context, outliers can be simply an error in the data records or an error generated from the processing of raw data. In other context which we will discuss in this book, is when the outliers hold valuable information that helps understand certain patterns.

Let's take again the example of peak flows. If we detect an abnormal high spring peak flow during a specific a year in a long record of flow timeseries covering several years, we might suspect that this peak flow is an outlier. However, before jumping into the conclusion that this flow is an error in the flow records, we might want to check if there are certain abnormal environmental process, such as high precipitation combined with a snowmelt caused by high temperatures, that has actually caused this high peak. In this case the detection of outliers may be handy to help understand the rare extreme weather events that might cause inundations. Outliers are detected based on patterns.

For instance, a fraudulent transaction can be detected based on the amount of the transaction and the place of transaction. These patterns are compared to the recorded previous patterns. Let's say for example a credit card or a bank account is stolen. The credit card company or the bank can detect the outliers or anomalies if an unusual transaction has occurred from the normal usage of the credit card or the bank account holder. The outlier detection is somewhat similar to clustering but it has a different goal. Instead of finding similar data points which is the goal of clustering, anomaly detection aims for detecting the unusual data point among a dataset.

The anomaly detection is very handy in different domains. For example, anomaly detection can be used to detect intrusion into a system. The way of connecting to a system, the network traffic can be considered as patterns to trigger a confidential level of a system and be assigned as an intrusion which a sort of anomaly detection. The fraudulent and suspicious transactions in banking and credit card systems are a direct application of anomaly detection.

In machine learning the anomaly detection can be classified into three categories namely *global or point, contextual* and collective. The global anomaly or point anomaly is a common anomaly detection. This type of anomaly detection aims at identifying data points that are far from the rest of the other data points. However, with this type of anomaly detection, it is challenging to determine at which distance from the rest of the data a point should be considered as an outlier. There is a lot of research on this subject.

One way to do so, is consider a distance from the normal or average of the data points. However, this assumption may not be the best approach if we consider several aspects or the context when this point occurred. Therefore, contextual anomaly detection can be useful. Indeed, contextual anomaly detection aims at detecting anomalies that occurs in a certain conditions or context. Let's consider again our example of temperature in Nordic countries.

Temperature above or around 20°C during winter in a Nordic country is an obvious temperature anomaly in this case. However, the same temperature in a southern country is normal. In this example, the location where the temperature is observed provide the context to consider a temperature record an anomaly or not. The collective anomaly detection is different than the other the global and contextual detections.

The collective anomaly detection aims at detecting the data points that occur together which from an anomaly. This data points sets are not necessarily anomalies if they are considered individually but the fact that they happened all together at once is the anomaly. For instance, in stock market, a price of a stock remains the same for a long period of time. It is usual that a price of a stock remains stable but it is expected to have some fluctuation over time. The fact that the price does not change over time is the anomaly. Now, that we understand the anomaly detection, let's see what algorithms can be used.

The are numerous methods to apply an anomaly detection. The simplest and direct method is to use a statistical based approach that consist of detecting points that largely diverge from the rest of the data points. The K-nearest neighborhood algorithm is another method that can be used. The nearest points are identified according to the Euclidean distance or the Mahalanobis distance. The k-means algorithm that we explored for clustering can also be used. For anomaly detection, data points that are not assigned to clusters formed by similar data points are considered anomalies.

Anomaly detection as we have explained in this section is very important in large different domains. The anomaly detection can be used for the verification of the performance of applications. The performance of an application may have a great impact on the productivity and the income generated by the application. It is very important to detect if their some inefficiencies and problems in the application as soon as they happen to react accordingly and fix the problem before it impacts the productivity and the income.

That is why the anomaly detection is important is this case to help detect anomalies within the application. The application can include the banking or trading platforms for example. The verification of the quality of products can also benefit from anomaly detection to help detect anomalies in a production system to prevent revenue losses.

The anomaly detection can be also used to improve user experience or detect anomalies in systems that provide user services such as the online business. System should be updated and maintained for an optimal user experience. Anomaly detection technics helps identify roots of problems and therefore an optimal interaction time to analyze the problem and solve it. Overall, the anomaly detection provides an automatic tool to perform a real-time verification and detection of a system failures.

This helps a fast and quick analysis of the root of problems which is beneficial to cut and prevent the losses as well as the damages that might be caused by these anomalies. The key elements to a successful anomaly detection are having large datasets to learn from as well as setting the optimal strategy to implement a supervised and unsupervised leaning to get the most information of the available data.

2.3 Semi-supervised learning

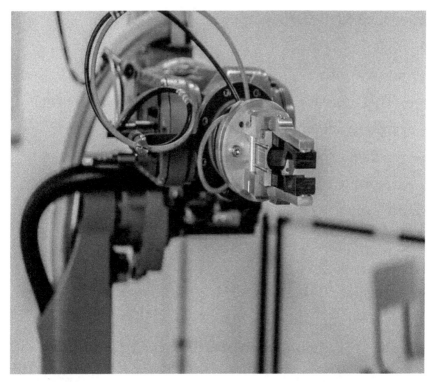

The semi-supervised learning is a hybrid approach that combines both supervised and unsupervised machine learning technics. It uses both labeled and unlabeled data. The semi-supervised learning is very hand when a mix of the labeled and unlabeled data are available. In real world application, the labeled data are not always available. So how does semi-supervised learning works?

Semi-supervised learning starts first by training the model on the labeled data. Then, it applies the trained model on the unlabeled data to generate more labeled data from these unlabeled data. This allows to build other model from the generated labeled datasets.

The pseudo learning a simplest method to do a semi-supervised learning. This process relies on the concept described above. It starts by training the model on the training dataset. Then it applies the model to predict the output of the unlabeled data. These outputs are merged with labels of the training dataset. The model is then fitted on the new formed data to enhance the model.

There are several semi-supervised learning algorithms. We cite the self-training algorithm, the multi-view algorithms, the graph-based algorithms and the generative models.

The self-trained algorithm consists of the same principle we presented before, where the model is trained on the labeled data, applied to predict the unlabeled data. Then the algorithm adds the predicted unlabeled data to the labeled data and repeats the same process. The self-training algorithm is the simplest and the most forward algorithm for the semi-supervised learning.

2.4 Reinforcement learning

Reinforcement learning is a different type of machine learning. This type of machine learning has different goals than the supervised and unsupervised learning. Reinforcement learning has the goal of optimizing a system in a certain context. It aims at finding the optimal strategies and actions to take in a contextual situation based on the feedback or a reward.

 Reinforcement is applicable only for certain problems. Games are an example of these problems. Reinforcement learning can be used to build wining strategies. The reinforcement algorithm tries to identify the best actions to take depending on several criteria in order to win the game. We will discuss these criteria later in this section. Now why reinforcement learning is important in some cases?

Reinforcement learning comes handy in order to automate the learning process and identify the best strategies to take. It helps learning and adapting its own behavior according to the feedback it gets from taking a specific action or decision. This learning allows building systems with little human expertise in the domain of the application. It also computationally efficient than building a model with series of rules to provide an optimal solution to the problem. Reinforcement learning can be applied in different domains. Like we stated before, it can be used to develop a game or more precisely logic games like chess or poker. It also handy in robotics engineering.

Reinforcement learning can be applied to develop a set of optimal motors to control a robot or robot navigation to learn behaviors of collision in order to prevent them. Now how do reinforcement learning algorithms work? Before jumping into that let's define the major components of a reinforcement learning components.

Reinforcement learning paradigm relies on seven concepts or components namely *environment, agent, action, state, reward, policy* and finally *value*. The *agent* is the core component of the reinforcement learning. An agent is the part of the learning paradigm that take actions. It can be an algorithm that models a concept or an algorithm that simulates a logic game for example.

Action is the combination of all possible moves or decisions that an algorithm can take.

These actions are usually pre-defined and the reinforcement algorithm choses among all these possible actions. In we take again our example of games, actions can be the directions that a player can take like moving right, left, up, down. These actions can also include the pace and speed of moving like jump, fast or slow or more the speed range values. *State* is the current condition where the agent is in which can be a specific location or moment that locate the agent in relation with other elements within its environment.

Reward is the feedback that agent receives from taking an action. The reward tells whether the action taken by the agent is successful or failure. Basically, the reward is a measure of how successful the action performed by the agent is. The reward is the objective function that the reinforcement learning algorithm is to optimize. *Environment* is the work domain where the agent operates. Generally, the environment is a procedure that process the action and the state of the agent. The environment evaluates the reward according to the state of the agent and the action made by the agent. According on the evaluated reward, the environment provides the next state of the agent.

Policy is a plan or a scheme that agent follows to determine the next action to take considering its current state. Policies assign actions to states of the agent in order to map the series of wining or rewarding actions. Finally, the *value* is a possible reward that the agent would have obtained it if have taken an action in a specific state. So how reinforcement algorithms optimize a system relying on these components?

The agent starts by making an action in a specific state. The environment evaluates this action and returns a reward and a state of the agent. Based on this state and reward the agent will take another action.

This process is repeated iteratively to allow to the agent to take a series of actions in different states. An optimal series of actions assigned to all state which forms a policy is defined once all the states and actions are performed numerous times. Basically, the algorithm tries to identify the best sequence of actions according to the state of the agent that should be taken in order to maximize the reward.

There are two schemes of reinforcement learning. The reinforcement learning can be positive or negative. The positive reinforcement aims at increasing the frequency of an action if a state or a reward occurs every time this action is taken. The negative reinforcement learning in the other hand, aims at decreasing the frequency of an action if a reward is not received or avoided.

Tow algorithms are widely used for reinforcement learning namely State- Action- Reward- Action and Q-learning algorithm. These algorithms usually use a neural network as the agent to improve their performance. Indeed, neural network are used to solve lot of machine learning algorithms. In the next chapter we will learn the basics and fundamentals of artificial neural networks.

Chapter 3: Artificial Neural Networks

Artificial neural networks are the craze of today's era. They are widely used in machine learning and Artificial intelligence. Moreover, they become an active research domain to improve their performance and be applied for large applications. So now you are wondering what are artificial neural networks?

How they work? How can you build an artificial neural network to solve a complex problem? We will answer all these question in this chapter of the book. Now let's first understand what is an artificial neural network and what is the main idea behind using this concept in machine learning.

3.1 Fundamentals of artificial neural network

Artificial neural networks are inspired from the human brain functioning. They emulate how the human learns. The artificial neural network is composed of several neurons that are connected to ach other. Each neuron is responsible of learning a part of the problem and afterwards they communicate that information to produce a final output. The artificial neural network works as black box, meaning that how they produce and they learn are not fully understood.

Typically, an artificial neural network is composed of an input layer and an output layer and one or more hidden layers. The input layer constitutes the input data that are fed to the neural network. The output layer is the target or the desired output. The hidden layer(s) are where the input data processed. These layers or layer is composed of several neurons.

So, what is a neuron in artificial neural network and how do we build an artificial neural network from several neurons? How do we connect all these neurons in layers? In this section we will answer these questions and we will explain in details the terminology used in artificial neural networks and their architecture.

Let's start first by the definition of neuron the core element in the network. A neuron a is simple mathematical function that sums the weighted inputs. Let's say for example we have M inputs of data that forms the vector $X = \{x_1, x_2, ..., x_m\}$ where x_i is a point element of the data. A neuron is the linear combination of all inputs given by the equation below:

$F(X) = \{x_1, x_2, ..., x_M\} = w_1 * x_1 + w_2 * x_2 + ... + w_M * x_M$; where w_i is the weight attributed to each input.

Now the input data X can be in the form of a matrix where each x_i is a vector of data features. In other words, each observation of the input data is a vector of features. The neuron can be expressed in matrix form such that:

$F(X) = W * X$; with W is a weight matrix.

So, basically a neuron is a linear function that is fed by input data to this neuron and returns a single output value. The weights are the parameters of the neuron. When we talk about training an artificial neural network, we are talking about estimating the matrix weight matrix W that provides a very high accurate output that the most similar to the desired or expected output. So, the weights are what differentiate each neuron from the other. We will see later in this chapter how to define the weights for each neuron.

Now, the neuron is a liner function of inputs to this neuron. But not only that, a neuron applies a non-linear function on top of the value returned by linear function. This non-linear function is called an activation function. So, to sum up a neuron is a weighted sum of the inputs with an applied activation function. Let's denote an activation function G. So, our formula for a neuron becomes:

G [F (X)] = G [**W** * **X**]; with **W** is a weight matrix and **X** the inputs.

The activation function determines if that neuron should be fired (i.e. activated) or not based on the model predictions. The activation function is crucial element of artificial neural network and should be carefully chosen. It has a great impact on the artificial neural network output.

We will go in more details in the next section about the activation functions that can be used within artificial neural networks and how each one works. So now the question is how do we build a network from these non-linear functions which represents several the neurons?

An artificial neural network is simply a mathematical function that connects all neurons together. So, what do we mean by connecting neurons? Let's look at the example of artificial neural network presented in the figure below:

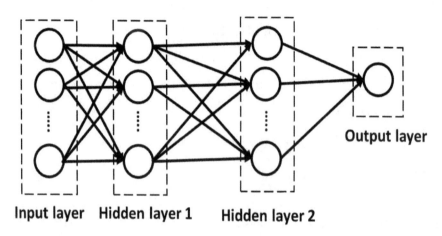

Input layer   **Hidden layer 1**   **Hidden layer 2**   **Output layer**

Example of artificial neural network

In the figure, we see that we have 4 layers. The first and the last are resp. the input and output layer. Neurons in the input layers are not mathematical functions like the one we explained before. These neurons are simply the input data we feed the artificial neural network.

The computation starts from the hidden layer 1. Looking at the two in-layers or hidden layers 1 and 2, we can see that the input from each neuron is fed to all other neurons in the next layers. This is what it means connecting the neurons. The final layer, the output layer takes as input values produced by the previous layer and produce a final output value.

This neuron is computed using similar equation we described before. In the final output layer, we are typically interested in a probability value between 0 and 1. For example in classification problem, we want a probability of input to belong to a specific class.

Hence, we use a non-linear function that is bounded by 0 and 1. In the next section we will see what activation functions satisfy this condition. In short, an artificial neural network is a non-linear function that is applied to a linear function applied to a non-linear function. This might seem complicated now. To better explain it and make it clear let's take the example of the artificial neural network in the figure above and explicitly understand the output from each layer.

We said the input layer does not contain any neuron in the sense of the mathematical explanation we provided for neurons. These are just data fed to the artificial neural network. So, the second layer computes the linear of the inputs. That is, if we have for example 5 neurons in the hidden layer 1. We have for each neuron G [F (X)] = X * **W**. So, in the second layer, each neuron is fed the output value of all neurons of hidden layer 1. That is for each neuron we have: $G[F(X_1)] = G(x11 * w11, x12 * w12, x13 * w13, x14 * w14, x15 * w15)$ where x_{1i} is the output from the neuron i in hidden layer 1 and the w_{1i} is the weight associated to it.

The output layer does the same calculation for the second hidden layer. If we have for example 5 neurons in the hidden layer 2, the output is: $G2[F(X_1)] = G2(x21 * w21, x22 * w22, x23 * w23, x24 * w24, x25 * w25)$ where x_{2i} is the output from the neuron i in hidden layer 2 and the w_{2i} is the weight associated to it and G2 is the non-linear activation function.

So, if we write the formula compacted for all layers, we have the final output as:
$Y = G2[F2[G1(F1(X), ..., F5(X)), ..., G5(F1(X), ..., F5(X)]]$
where the G2 and F2 the non-linear function and linear function applied in the hidden layer 2 respectively. The G1 and F1 are the non-linear and linear functions applied in the hidden layer 1. F1 and F2 are different because the weights **W** is different. The formula given above is for an example of layers composed of 5 neurons.

To summarize, artificial neural network computes the output using an activation function that is applied to each output layer which is the weighted sum of the inputs to that layer. In order to define an artificial neural network, we need to define the number of hidden layers, the number of neurons per hidden layer.

That is what defines the structure or architecture of the artificial neural network. We also need to define the activation function and the weights associated to each neuron for each layer. These weights are defined in the training process and fixed when the artificial neural is tested. Other parameters should be defined in the process of training the artificial neural network. We will discuss those parameters later in this chapter when explaining how to train an artificial neural network. Now let's discover how do we choose and define the activation function one of the most important elements in an artificial neural network?

3.2 Activation functions in artificial neural network

Activation functions are the crucial component of an artificial neural network that make the decisions of activating or not a neuron. The activation function has the role of evaluating the output of each neuron and deciding if that output value should be considered or connected to the other neurons. If take back the definition of a neuron. A neuron is linear combination or the sum of the weighted inputs to that specific neuron.

The neuron does not have any information on how reasonable that values is or what are the acceptable ranges for that value.

So, the activation function is the function that provide that information within an artificial neural network. It checks the output of each neuron of the network. There are a wide variety of activation function that can be used.

We cite the *step function*, *linear activation function*, the *logistic* or the *sigmoid function*, the *tanh function*, the *Rectified Linear Unit function* and the *softmax function*. These are the most commonly activation functions used. Indeed, lot of research applications are interested in defining optimal activation function to implement in artificial neural networks.

The *step function* is the simplest and most intuitive activation function. As we explained before activation function decides whether to activate or not a neuron within an artificial neural network. The step function is based on the simple idea of fixing a threshold. Based on this threshold, the neuron is active or not. For instance, if the output value of the neuron is above that fixed threshold than the neuron is activated and it is less than that threshold it is not activated. Mathematically if consider Y is the output of a neuron, the step function is defined as follows:

F = 'activate neuron' or F = 1, if Y is above the threshold.

F = 'do not activate neuron', or F = 0, if Y is less than threshold.

The step function is very handy for classification problems that expect a binary output as Yes or No (i.e. 0 or 1). Although the step function is straightforward and easy to understand it has a downside. The main downside of this function is its inability to distinguish between different classes for a classification problem.

For example, we are faced with a classification problem where we have data that might belong to more than two classes. Because the step function only takes values 0 or 1, if more than one neuron is activated in the network the final output will be 1 for all output meaning that all inputs will belong to a single class.

Or simply it will be hard to tell to which class each input belongs to because 1 means that they belong to a certain class. In short, the step function cannot handle multiple output values or classification into more than one or two classes.

The *linear function* is an alternative function that provides a wide range of values unlike the step function. The linear function estimates an output that is proportional to the input to the layer. The fact that this function is linear makes it not very useful in lot of applications.

First of all, the linear function does not provide any information on which input has more weight. It does not allow backpropagation for the artificial neural network. In other words, the derivative or gradient of the linear function is always a constant which is the weight matrix W. Therefore, when training the model, we are not able identify the what changes on the input to the neuron improve the model performance because the gradient of the linear function is completely independent from changes into the input X of the neuron.

Another downside of the linear function is that not matter how many layers we use in an artificial neural network they all can be reduced to a single layer, because a combination of linear functions is a linear function. So the final output is the same is as the linear combination of the first layer and the in between layers do not have any utility, which contradict the core idea behind artificial neural network that relies on the fact the more hidden layers you might be able to improve the performance of the artificial neural network.

Overall, an artificial neural network connected by linear activation function is nothing more than a linear regression unable to handle the complex structure in the data. In fact, numerous or all almost all real applications or problem are non linear problems. The relationship that relates the inputs to the outputs is non linear and for that we need non-linear function.

The non-linear function is able to map the hidden complex structures in the data. Hence, the non-linear activation functions are more useful within an artificial neural network and allow the network to learn the complex patterns in the data and in particular in high dimensional data like images or audios.

The derivative or gradient of non-linear function always depends on the input X therefore it relies on the changes in X. Therefore, they allow for backpropagation in artificial neural network. They also support several hidden layers in an artificial neural network.

Several non-linear activation functions can be implemented within an artificial neural network. In this book we will cover the commonly used ones namely the *sigmoid function*, the *tanh function*, the *softmax function* and *Rectified Linear Unit function*.

The *sigmoid function* is a commonly used as activation function in artificial neural networks. This function takes values between 0 and 1. The mathematical formulations of this function is as given below:

$$F(X) = 1/ (1 + \exp (-X))$$

The sigmoid function is the inverse of the exponential of X plus 1. When values of X are above 2 or under -2, the values of the output of this function are close to extreme values 0 and 1. The figure below presents the curve of the sigmoid function. As we can see from the figure that for all values above 4 and under -4, the output Y or the value of the sigmoid function is around 0 and 1.

There is a small change to almost a non-significant change of the sigmoid function evaluated for values outside the range of -4 and 4. This issue is what is called the '*vanishing gradient*'. The vanishing gradient means that the gradient is very small on the extreme part of the sigmoid function.

The vanishing gradient problem is major downside of the sigmoid function which the learning process of artificial neural network very slow when they get close to the edges of the function. This has an impact on the computational efficiency making it very expensive.

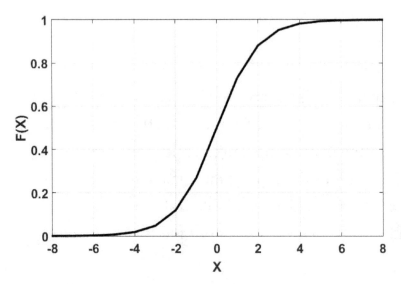

Sigmoid activation function.

The *tanh function* has some similarities with the sigmoid function and also suffers from the same issue of vanishing gradient. However, the tanh function takes values between -1 and 1 with a more pronounced gradient than the sigmoid function. This function is zero centered which makes is very handy when inputs can be negative, positive or neutral. The tanh function is expressed mathematically as follows:

$$F(X) = \tanh(X) = [2 / (1 + \exp(-2 * X)] - 1.$$

The *Softmax function* is a different activation function that comes handy when we face a classification problem into several classes. This function computes the probability of an input to belong into a certain class. It normalizes outputs of each category to have values between 0 and 1. It then divides the value for each output by the sum of all values to provide the probability for each input to belong to different categories.

The *Rectified Linear Unit* function is conventionally called the *ReLU* function. This function is the most widely used function among the activation functions cited in this section. This function is computationally efficient and allows overcoming the problems faced when using the sigmoid function or the tanh function described before in this section. The ReLU function has a very simple mathematical formulation:

$$F(X) = \max(0, X).$$

The ReLU function is basically the identity function when X is positive and is 0 when the input X is negative. So, the ReLU function takes values from 0 to +inf. The ReLU function does not have an upper bound. The shape of the ReLu function might seem similar to a shape of a linear function, but the ReLU function supports a gradient.

The only the drawback of the ReLU function is that gradient is null for all input values that are negative. Like for the linear function, the backpropagation cannot be performed when the input values are negative. The neural network is only able to learn on the condition that the input values are positive. The fact that of the gradient is null when inputs are negative is called dying ReLU.

Other variations of the ReLu have been proposed to prevent the dying ReLU problem. The *Leaky ReLU function* is one variation we cite in this book. The leaky ReLU is defined as the identity function if the input values of X are positive and as 0.1*X if the values of X are negative. Mathematically this function is given by the equation below:

$$F(X) = \max (0.1 * X, X)$$

The gradient of this function when the input values are negative is 0.1. That allows for backpropagation in the training process of the artificial neural network. But the predictions of negative values may not be very consistent. Another variation of the ReLU is the parametric ReLU. This function relies on the same concept of the leaky ReLU. It adds a pre-defined parameter as a gradient when the input values are negative. The parametric function is the identity function when the inputs are positive. When the input values are negative the parametric ReLU is the pre-defined parameter by the value of the input. This function is as follows:

$$F(X) = \max (a * X, X)$$

Other variations of ReLU exist like the *exponential linear ReLU*. This function has a log curve function when the input values are negative. This might be a positive side of the exponential ReLU compared to the other variations of the ReLU that we cited. The leaky and the parametric ReLU functions have a linear function when inputs are negative.

However, the exponential ReLU might saturate when the negative values are very large which is a downside of this function. Other variations of the ReLU function exists. They all rely on the same concept that is defining a non-null gradient for the function when the inputs values are negative.

Now you are probably wondering how to choose an activation function to use within an artificial neural network given that there is no perfect function and each one has its pros and cons. In short there is no guidance how to choose an activation function. It all depends on the problem you are trying to solve. Better understanding what to expect from the neural network and the problem that you have in hand will guide towards an activation function or other one.

If the characteristics of the target function to estimate is somewhat know beforehand that should help choosing an activation. For example, the sigmoid function or the Softmax activation function are a good choice for classification problems. In general, it is recommended to start with the ReLU activation function.

Then you can try other activation functions until you reach a satisfactory neural network. ReLU is applicable for a wide range of applications or better you can try defining your own activation function. The key is to go through a trial and error process in order to better build an efficient neural network. It is an ongoing active research area and still there is no clear guidance on the subject of choosing an activation function.

However, there is an aspect that is very important to count for when choosing an activation function which is sparsity. Sparsity means that the activation function does not activate all neurons at once. This characteristic is very desired in an activation function implemented within an artificial neural network because it allows for neural network to learn faster. It also decreases the probability of a trained artificial neural network to be overfitted.

Let's say for example we dispose of an artificial neural network with numerous neurons which is generally the case. If all neurons are activated then they are all processed to the final output. In this case, the network becomes very dense and decreases the computational efficiency of the neural network. The ReLU function has the sparsity characteristic which makes very efficient and that is why it is recommended to start trying this function first then move to other activation function if the results are not satisfactory.

The sigmoid and the tanh activation functions are not very inefficient because they tend to activate almost all neurons. Therefore, they are not sparse functions. Now you have learnt how an artificial neural network works and the principal components of an artificial neural network. So how can we build a neural network or more precisely how the layers are structured?

To answer to these questions let's explore in the next section the type of artificial neural networks that exist and when they are applicable.

3.3 Types of artificial neural networks

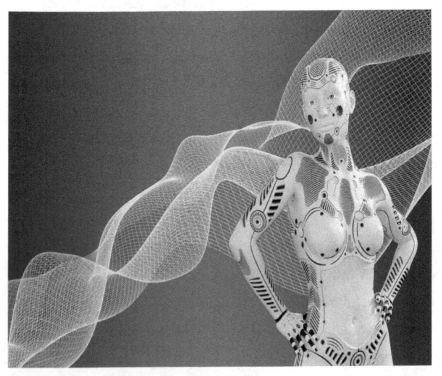

There are different types of artificial neural networks to choose from. Each type has specific properties and a certain level of complexity which makes it applicable for certain problematics. In this book we will cover the most common used ones which are the *feedforward neural networks, recurrent neural networks, multi-layer neural networks, convolutional neural networks,* and *modular neural networks.*

Perceptron and feedforward neural networks

First let's start by the original and the simplest artificial neural network developed which is the perceptron. All types of artificial neural networks that exist and the ones we will describe in this book all rely on the concept of the perceptron. We can view them as several perceptron with different characteristics connected all together.

The perceptron was first introduced by Frank Rosenblatt in the 50s. The perceptron is a single neuron that is fed by the input data and applies a sigmoid function. In a simplified way, the perceptron computes the weighted sum of the input data and returns a value of 0 or 1 depending on the value of the weighted sum of inputs.

Conventionally, if the weighted sum is negative the perceptron returns 0 and if the weighted sum if positive the perceptron returns 1. In general, the perceptron is only applicable if it used to classify linear binary problems because it uses a sigmoid function and returns only 1 or 0 also it is based on a single neuron.

The feedforward neural network relies on the simple concept of the perceptron that has one layer. This type of neural networks is among the first neural networks developed and used. The feedforward neural network as its name indicates, propagates the information in a single direction which is from the input layer to the output layer.

This procedure of passing the information from the input to the output through the hidden layers is called the front propagated wave that is based on the information provided by the activation function. The feedforward neural network is composed of a hidden layer of several neurons that are fully connected.

The output layer of this type of neural network is the value of the activation function applied to the weighted sum of inputs to the hidden layer. Backpropagation method is usually used to train such type of neural network. The logistic or sigmoid function is an activation function that is typically used within a feedforward neural network.

The feedforward neural network has been developed through the years and numerous derivations of this type of neural networks exist now. The radial basis function neural is one derivation of the feedforward neural network. This derivation uses the radial basis function as an activation function instead of the logistic function.

The radial function is a measure of distance to the center. In other words, the radial function provides the distance of each point to the relative center of all data points. Unlike the logistic function that allows mapping arbitrary binary values, the radial function provides continuous values that allows measuring the distance from the desired value.

Typically, the radial basis function neural network, has two layers. Neurons in the inner layer are connected by the radial basis function. Deep feedforward neural networks are another variation of feedforward neural network. This type of artificial neural network is composed of several hidden layers. A new learning has immerged from this type of neural network called deep learning. The deep learning became a whole separate branch and active research domain in artificial intelligence and machine learning.

 The deep feedforward neural networks yield to better results than a basic feedforward neural network. However, there are some challenges to implement a deep neural network regarding the optimal number of hidden layers to use as well as training the neural network.

Indeed, having more hidden layers is advantageous to get better results but the question of how many layers are enough remains.

The number of the hidden layers should also be optimized in this type of neural networks.

The feedforward neural networks are able to learn from training datasets. They provide an output depending on the value of the input. In some systems, we are interested in the value of the output knowing the value of the input but also according to the value of the previous output or depending on the value of the previous input.

For example, in timeseries, the output in a timestep i will depend not only on the input on timestep i but also on the output at time timestep i-1. Let's take another example speech recognition. To interpret a sequence of words in a context, the word's meaning or reference in a sequence will depend on the previous words in the sequence. This is normally how the human brain works. When you start interpreting something your interpretation along your reading depends on how you interpret or understand the previous elements.

You don't start from nothing at each element. The feedforward neural networks are unable to emulate this process of learning, simply because the information is processed in a single direction which is from the input to the output. So, there is an obvious need of a structured neural network that processes the output too. Here comes the advantage of *recurrent neural networks* to address this issue.

Recurrent neural networks

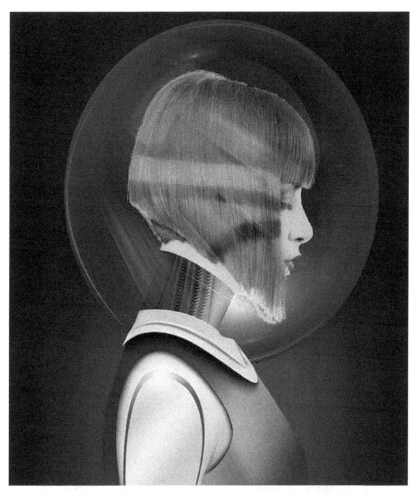

Recurrent neural networks are a category of artificial neural networks that take as input timeseries or any series that are structured within time framework or a space framework. They process information like the feedforward neural network from the input layer to the output layer. They however process information from the output layer to the input layer. That is the recurrent neural networks process the information in two directions.

They use a memory at each node to save the output that is processed back to the input layer. So, the recurrent networks output is always impacted by its output from the past. They not only learn from the input training set but also from the previous decisions they make in the past. The recurrent neural through the memory implemented in the network they have a state vector that provides a context to process the input.

This state vector or context is updated according to the input. So similar inputs may yield to different outputs according to the state of previous input in the sequence forming the input layer. In short, the recurrent neural network maps the relationship between the output, the input as well as the relationship within the inputs. So, at each time step, the input to a hidden layer h is a function as follows $h_t = G (W * X_t + Uh_{t-1})$, where X_t is the input at time step t and W is the same weight used at the feedforward and as explained before and Uh_{t-1} is the hidden state at the previous iteration.

The G function is an activation function that can be either a sigmoid activation function or the tanh activation function.

There are different categories of recurrent neural networks that relies on the same principle of using other information than the inputs to produce the output. For instance, the *bidirectional recurrent neural networks*. This category of recurrent neural network uses the future possible output to predict the present output.

Let's consider speech recognition, it might better to consider the whole sequence to provide an interpretation of a word in a sequence. Interpreting a word based on previous words might leave some ambiguity, but include the next words in the sequence might remove that ambiguity and better interpret the present word. *Recursive neural networks* are a broad form of recurrent networks. The shape of this category of neural network is more like a tree shape.

The hierarchical tree is formed by the inputs where each node (parent) is connected to other child node which lead to other child nodes. The recursive neural networks are very complex and computationally exhaustive. Another variation of recurrent neural networks is the *Sequence to Sequence recurrent neural network*. This class of neural network typically uses two recurrent networks where one is used to save updates in the hidden state and provide the final state output. This first network is called the encoder.

The second recurrent neural network process the information provided by the encoder in order to produce the final output. This neural network is called the decoder. In short, the encoder recurrent neural network encodes the context of the inputs and the decoder translate that information into formal output. Here, the size of the output sequence should be the same as the size of the input sequence, unlike the other recurrent neural network where there is no limitation of the input size. *Long Short-Term Memory* is another class of recurrent neural networks.

The Long Short-Term Memory was introduced by the two researchers Sepp Hochreiter and Jürgen Shmidhuber to solve the problem of the vanishing gradient issue in recurrent neural networks. Remember the vanishing gradient happens when the gradient is no longer calculated or becomes null when the iteration goes through which does not allow updating the parameters and hence does not allow for the model to learn. The Long Short-Term memory help save the error which can be processed by backpropagation in time as well through each layer of the neural network.

The Short Long Term allows as stated by the authors to the neural network to learn after two many times steps and over 1000 iterations. This is very common in machine learning algorithms and artificial neural networks where learning requires lot of iterations to learn. Unlike recurrent neural networks, the Long Short-Term Memory support saving information for over long iteration (i.e. period of time). The Long Short-Term Memory can be applied for prediction of time series or classification according to time series datasets.

The Long Short-Term Memory has a different structure than the other recurrent neural networks. It has a structure of a chain that has 4 neural networks with implemented cells that are called memory blocks. The Long Short-Term Memory uses also the concept of gates to manipulate the memory. The gates serve to control the information contained in the cell so we call it a gated cell. The Long Short-Term Memory uses three types of gates that allows saving, writing or reading information from a cell.

These gates act like neurons meaning they multiply inputs by weights and apply a sigmoid or tanh function to make decision about saving, removing or reading the information according to strength of the information. The weights like for neurons are adjusted during the learning process of the network. Therefore, cells also learn when to store in information, read out the information or delete the information during the training process of the neural network by back propagation.

The three type of gates that are used to control the information the flows in and out a cell are the *forget gate*, the *input gate* and the *output gate*. The forget gate, as its name indicates, removes the information which is not needed or not useful any more in the cell. This gate takes two inputs which are X_t the input at the timestep t and H_{t-1} is the precedent output of the cell.

These inputs are fed to the forget gate weighted by a parameter matrix. An activation function returning 0 or 1 like the sigmoid activation function is applied to the resultant value. If the value of the cell is 0 than the information is removed and if the value is 1 then the information is kept for the eventual use in the following iterations. In fact, the forget gate can be viewed as a linear identity function.

The reason for that is when the gate is open, the information is processed forward for another iteration or time step by multiplying the current memory cell state by 1. The second type of gates used is the input gate. This gate adds helpful information to the cell state. Like the forget gate, the input X_t at the current step and H_{t-1} is the precedent output of the cell are fed to the input gate.

Then the sigmoid activation function is applied to the value and the information to be saved is selected. Afterwards, the tanh function is applied to create all plausible values out of H_{t-1} and X_t. These plausible values are stored in a vector as values from ranging from -1 to 1.

Finally, these plausible values are multiplied by the regulated values in order to get that helpful information. The third type of gates used by the Long Short-Term Memory is the output gate. This gate is responsible of drawing helpful information that should be processed from the current state of the cell. Using the tanh function on the current state of the cell, this gate generates a vector.

This vector is then filtered via the sigmoid function to decide which values should be retained taking as input the current state of the cell X_t and the previous state of the cell H_{t-1}. Finally, the vector values and the output values from the sigmoid function are multiplied and processed as an output and fed to following cell. So how these gates communicate and work within a cell of the Long Short Term? The first thing the Long Short-Term Memory does in a cell at a time step is taking decisions about which information should be dumped from the cell state. So, it applies the forget gate process.

Then, it takes decisions about which new information should be saved in the state of the cell. In this step the Long Short-Term Memory applies the two-step process of the input gate. Finally, it takes decisions about which information should be processed forward or what information should be processed to the output.

At this state the Long Short-Term Memory applies the processes of the output gate. So, to summarize the gated cell takes as input the previous state of the cell H_{t-1} and the current input X_t. These inputs are processed through the three gates that are applied in the following order forget gate, input gate and output gate. These gates work the same way as neurons and have their own weights that are adjusted during the learning process.

There are several variants of the Long Short-Term Memory that were introduced in different research papers. We cite in this book the gated recurrent unit, Long Short-Term Memory with peephole connections, depth Gated Recurrent neural networks. The gated recurrent unit variant does not use an output gate.

Hence, the information contained in the memory cell is processed to the full network without filter at every time step.

The Long Short-Term Memory with peephole connections adds a peephole connection that allows the gates of the cell to consider the state of the cell.

Other variants of the Long Short-Term Memory include coupling the forget gate with the input gate. So, the gated cells of this variant make decisions about what information should be dropped and what information should be added at the same time, instead of making these decisions in a separate manner. So, the cell adds input to the state of the cell only if new information is being forgotten. In the same way, the cell forgets an existing information only if a new information is going to be added at its spot.

Convolutional neural networks

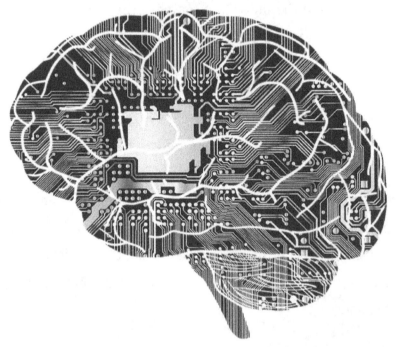

Convolutional neural networks are a branch or artificial neural network that is based on the concept of convolution. Before we diving in this type of artificial neural network, let's find out what is convolution first. Mathematically speaking convolution is a function that takes two functions or signals and produce a new signal.

The convolution function is the multiplication of two functions that are fed to this convolution function. In neural networks convolution is simply an application of a filter to the input in order to activate this input. The convolution multiplies the inputs data with weights. Now you think this the same concept a regular neural network. Indeed, it is similar to the operation done in regular neural network. However, the convolution takes two-dimensional input and the weights here a two-dimensional array.

This multiplication is called a filter. Applying the same filter several times produces a map of activations that is commonly nominated as a feature map. This feature map provides an indication of how powerful a feature is and its location within inputs. The convolution neural networks are very handy when it comes to processing images.

Image is a raster or matrix. We can actually convert that matrix into a vector and feed it to regular feedforward neural network for classification. However, the feedforward neural networks are not able to map the dependencies of space and time in the image. Because the convolutional network uses the convolution concept and applies filters, they are powerful to map the dependencies in an image. The image is fed as a matrix to the convolutional neural network.

Remember the convolutional neural network takes as input multi-dimensional input. The convolutional neural network reshapes the image or matrix into by decreasing its size into easier form by conserving the major features that have more weights and crucial to produce accurate estimations.

The layer where the convolution is done is called the convolutional layer. The convolution has the goal of detecting the important features in an image like edges, colors. A convolutional neural network can contain several convolutional layers. Now how the convolutional neural networks work and how do they use the convolution operation? We will answer these questions in details in the rest of this section.

Convolutional networks perform four major operations which the convolution we cited before and what makes them special, non-linearity as all neural network types, Sub sampling or what is called pooling in the terminology of convolutional neural networks, and finally classification. These tasks are the very basic elements in any convolutional network. So, let's go through each task in details. To do so, we consider here an example of an image.

Remember an image can be represent simply by a matrix of values where each value is a pixel value. Conventionally a channel is used to point toward a specific feature of an image. Images have 3 channels where each channel represents blue, green and red. These channels can be represented by 3 of 2-

dimensional matrices of pixel values between 0 and 255 assembled on each other.

Typically, grayscale images are represented only by one channel because they don't have any colors other than the black and white. A pixel value of 0 represents the black and a pixel value of 255 represents white. The grayscale images can be represented by one single matrix of 2 dimensions. For simplicity, we will consider a grayscale image to explain the convolutional network functioning. Hence, we consider a matrix I of 6 by 6 dimension where values are between 0 and 255. To apply the convolution operation, we consider a second 4 by 4 matrix F.

This matrix is what is called the filter or kernel in the convolutional networks. In fact, the second matrix slides over the first matrix that represents our image and apply element multiplication of the two matrices. The resultant matrix is conventionally nominated as the Activation map or Convolved feature.

For instance, we denote the Activation map matrix as A. The first element A (1, 1) of the Activation map A is computed as the multiplication of F and I (1:4, 1:4), where I (1:4, 1:4) is the sub matrix of I that contains the four first rows and the four first columns. Then, the second element A (1, 2) is computed as the multiplication of I (1:4, 2:5) and F. Basically, the matrix F is sliding by one pixel over the image.

The number of pixels by which the matrix is sliding is called stride. So now you probably must be thinking that setting up different filter values will provide different Activation maps and probably you are wondering how we can fixe the values of the filter matrix? Yes, indeed different filter matrices applied to the same input image will provide different Activation maps. These filters are adjusted in the training process. In other words, the convolutional neural networks will learn the filter values via the training.

The challenge in implementing a convolutional neural network include the number of filters to use and the dimensions of the filter matrix. Here we just presented a random filter example. But to apply a convolutional neural network the size of the filter should be wisely fixed. Regarding the number of filters, higher number of filters implemented means that more features are going to be pulled from the image and the performance of the to recognize images is increasing.

The dimension of the Activation Map is dictated by three factors which should be fixed prior to performing the convolution. These factors are the stride, the depth, and the zero-padding.

The stride as we explained before represents the number of pixels according to which the filter matrix is sliding.

For instance, if the stride is 1 then the filter is sliding by only one pixel as the example presented above. If the stride is 3, then the filter will move by 3 pixels each time it is sliding. As general rule the smaller stride is the more feature are mapped. The depth represents the number of filters that are being used to perform the convolution task. Each filter will produce a different Activation Map.

These Activation Maps can be assembled on each other to provide a Nd matrix. The depth hence would be N. The zero-padding allows to apply a buffer around the edges in order to be able to perform convolution operation on the edges of the images. Once the convolution operation is performed, an activation function is applied. It can be an ReLu, the sigmoid or the tanh functions.

However, it is recommended to use the ReLu because it provides the best results. The application of the activation function adds the non-linearity to the convolutional neural network. This step provides a rectified Activation Map. The third step is the sub sampling or the pooling operation. The sub sampling consists of performing a dimension reduction of the Activation Map.

This operation is done by retaining only the most useful information. Different sub sampling can be used like the sum, average or max among of others. The sub-sampling is done according to pre-fixed spatial zone that is defined like a filter and a stride. Let's say for example we do a sub-sampling using the average.

We can define a spatial zone as 2 by 2 matrix. So, we go through each 2 by 2 block of the Rectified Activation Map and take the average value of the block. For example, we have 6 by 6 Rectified Activation Map Denoted R. The sub sampling is performed by computing the average of the R (1:2,1:2), R(1:2, 3:4) and so on for each block of 2 by 2 of the Rectified Activation Map. This reduces the dimension of the map of features. The sub sampling is applied to all Activation Maps that were produced through the different filters applied to the input image.

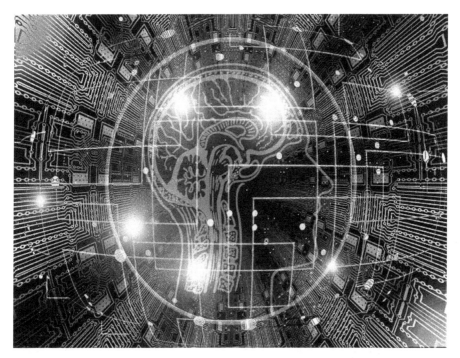

The pooling or sub sampling has several functions which are reducing the dimension of the features of the image in order to make it easy to manage, making the network stable and invariant to small changes in the input image, making the network less prone to overfitting by reducing the number of parameters, it conserve the representation of the image and makes is easy to extract objects wherever they are placed within the image.

After the convolutional operation and the sub sampling, the results from the sub sapling are outputted and used for image classification. All the features resulted from the convolution and the sub sampling are connected as multi layer feedforward network. The SoftMax activation is applied to the resulted output and produce a vector of values where the sum is equal to 1.

So, to summarize the convolution and the sub sampling helps extracting and identifying the major important features of an image and the last layer defined as a feedforward network acts as the classifier. The convolutional neural network is trained similarly as the feedforward neural networks using feedforward and back propagation. In the convolutional neural network, filters are adjusted in addition to the weights.

Modular neural networks

Modular neural networks combine several neural networks that are connected to each other. Each neural network is responsible of solving a specific problem that forms a complex problem. In other words, the major complex problem is subdivided into sub-problems to be handled by each neural network that form the modular neural network. Hence, the combine strength of a combination of neural networks to tackle a complex problem. Basically, the idea behind modular neural network is 'divide and conquer'.

When you divide a problem, it is easier to solve each sub-problem separately. Now you have learnt the different types of artificial neural networks. Let's find out in the next section what are the advantages and disadvantages as well as the challenges of implementing an artificial neural network.

3.4 Pros and cons of an artificial neural network

The advantages of using artificial neural networks are the same as the advantages we listed for machine learning in the previous section. The are able to handle large datasets, do not require expertise and in-depth knowledge in domain they are applied to.

They can easily map complex structures in datasets. In addition, artificial neural networks are very flexible and can be applied for all kind of machine learning supervised, unsupervised and reinforcement learning.

As we learned from the types of artificial neural networks, the different architecture of artificial neural network allows them to be applied to predict the evolution of timeseries data using the recurrent neural network and Long Short-term memory, simple classification using the feedforward neural network, or image recognition using the convolutional neural networks.

Now you might be wondering what is the advantage of using artificial neural networks over the methods we presented in the previous section such us logistic regression or linear regression. The main advantage of using artificial neural network over these methods logistic and linear regression methods is that artificial neural networks does not require any statistical adjustment. In other words, artificial neural networks are a non-parametric approach. In addition, artificial neural networks do not require any assumptions regarding the distribution or structure of the data. Actually, you can consider artificial neural network as a regression applied on a multi-dimensional space.

If we consider back the example the regression example in previous section, we are trying to approximate a function $f(X)$ = W * **X** + B that provides the output **Y**. Now the artificial neural network does the same thing. Each neuron is the same as the function f. Remember the output of neuron is the weighted sum of input which is exactly the same function as f with B as bias.

Now you might think that artificial neural network is the same as linear regression. But don't' forget the artificial neural networks apply an activation function to this output. That is why artificial neural networks are able to solve non-linear problems. Moreover, artificial neural networks allow for parallel processing.

The major disadvantage of artificial neural network is that they operate as black-box. Indeed, they provide good results in the condition that they are applied correctly, but they cannot tell what is the exact relation between the input and the output or how they reach that specific decision. That means you cannot interpret the behavior of the neural network. Artificial neural networks are computationally exhaustive and hard to train.

The challenge of implementing an artificial neural network is making decision of the number of hidden layers as well as the number of neurons in each hidden layer. There is no guidance regarding the optimal number of hidden layers or the number of neurons per hidden layer. It takes experience and an error trial process to find out the optimal number of neurons and hidden layers to use in artificial neural network and define the optimal architecture.

Another challenge is to find the right activation function as well as the right optimization algorithm to train the artificial neural network. Hence, there are lot of choices and elements in the artificial neural network to adjust in order to find to best representation of your artificial neural network.

That might make the process very complex and time consuming. Moreover, artificial neural networks are only effective on large datasets. If the small dataset is available, it is better to use another alternative method. Artificial neural networks are prone to overfitting meaning that you can achieve a high performance on the training dataset.

But when the artificial neural network is applied on a similar independent dataset, that high performance drops drastically. Because artificial neural networks are better used and trained on large dataset, the training process might be very time consuming and computationally intensive. Parallel computing can be used but it might be a complex process to implement such computing.

3.5 *How to define and train an artificial neural network*

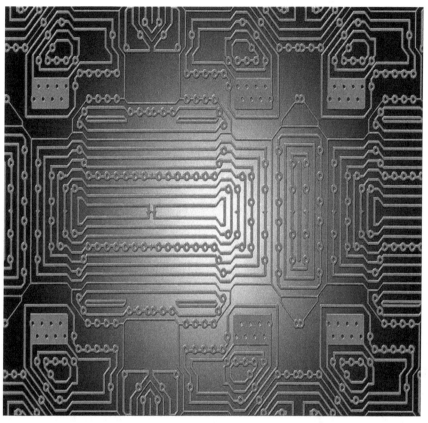

Let's summarize first what we have leant in this chapter about artificial neural networks and remember all components of a network. An artificial neural network is some non-linear function applied on a linear function which is weighted combination of the inputs.

Now each the linear function is what connects the neurons to each other and non-linear function, which is the activation function, is what gives the artificial neural network its non-linear ability to sole complex problems. So, in order to define an artificial neural network, we need to define the number of layers and the number of neurons for each layer. We also need to fix an activation function.

Once these elements are defined, we can think of the training process of the artificial neural network. Basically, we need to estimate the optimal weights of each neuron. The training process is an iterative procedure that implies running the artificial neural network.

Then evaluating the output provided according to some weights assigned to the neurons. Once the output is evaluated, we correct the weights based on the evaluation of the output. Then we re-run the artificial neural network with the corrected weights and so on until we achieve a good performance.

This process of going back and forth is called feedforward propagation and back propagation. We will explain these two processes in details later in this section. This iterative procedure of training the artificial neural network requires a definition of a loss or objective function as well as an optimization algorithm.

We also need three independent datasets to train and test the artificial neural network. Now that you can see the big picture and what is involved in defining and training an artificial neural network, let's dig in into each element. We will start by some rules to build an artificial neural network.

Rules to follow in building an artificial neural network

The number of neurons per layer and number of layers are important elements in artificial neural network. As we mentioned before there is no guidance on the optimal dimension to define an artificial neural network structure. It is a black art and depend on the expertise of the modeler.

However, there are some rules to follow that are recommended in the course of the years of applying artificial neural networks. In general, the number of neurons in the hidden layers should increase if the problem is complex and the relationship that relates the input data to the output data is complicated. That is if the number of feature data used to predict the output is high than the number of neurons should also be high.

The quantity of data to train the artificial neural network can be a good indicator of how many neurons can be used. In fact, it the quantity of the training dataset can provide a maximum bound of number of neurons to be used. To get an estimate of this maximum number, you can divide the number of elements you have in the training dataset by the number of neurons you have in the input as well as the output layer.

The computed ratio should be divided by a factor ranging from 5 to 10. In general, a small factor is applied for noisy data. The more hidden layers you have the more likely you increase the efficiency of the artificial neural network. Basically, if the problem being solved can be downsized into sub-problems or solved in several steps, then it is suited to add more layers. If the problem cannot be solved in several steps, then the extra-layers might just serve as a memory and do not add valuable addition in the artificial neural network.

In this case the artificial neural network is highly prone to overfitting which makes not applicable to data different than the training dataset. Overall, if you have dense network meaning too many neurons and too many layers, the higher is likely that the artificial neural network is prone to overfitting.

Data for training the artificial neural network

Data is also is an important element that dictates the performance of an artificial neural network. It is a crucial component to build an artificial neural network. Assuming that you pre-processed the data. In other, let's assume that you cleaned the data from any plausible outliers and converted the data into a format that is ready to be used by the neural network. Typically, you should split the data into three datasets. The first dataset that we call the training dataset is used to train the model using an optimization algorithm. The neural network optimal parameters i.e. weights are estimated using this training dataset.

Then, the neural network is applied to predict the output of the second dataset that we call the validation dataset. After evaluating the output of the validation dataset, if the results are not satisfactory, we train another time the neural network by changing some elements that can be the optimization algorithm, the model structure for example. Then once again the neural network is applied to the validation dataset to evaluate its accuracy.

We repeat the process until we reach a satisfactory performance. Note that in this process of using the training and validation dataset, the training process is not completely independent from the validation dataset. The reason for that is that we adjust some choice in the training process according the performance of the model on the validation dataset although this dataset is not used explicitly during the optimization. That is why we have a third training dataset that we call the test dataset.

This dataset is used once the artificial neural network is trained and the parameters as well as all the elements of the network are fixed and no other changes are to be made in the neural network. The evaluation of the neural network of predicting the test dataset output should proved an independent and objective accuracy evaluation of the neural network.

Loss function

Loss function or what is commonly called in optimization domain objective function is simply a mathematical function that measures or reflects how accurate a model prediction is. The most direct way to measure the efficiency of a model is to compute the difference between the model output and the actual target output. In short, the loss function reflects the model error. It evaluates a candidate set of parameters and returns a value that is the model error with respect to this parameterization.

The widely used loss function is the Mean Squared Error. This loss function is computed as the mean value of the differences between the target values and the estimated values. If Y_{act} and Y_{pred} are the actual true value and the predicted values resp., the Mean Square Error is: $L = (1/m) * (\sum (Y_{act} - Y_{pred})^2)$ where m is the number of observations of the output. The difference between the actual true value Y_{act} and the predicted output value Y_{pred} is called the residual. The returned value is always positive whether the difference between the target and the estimated values is positive or negative.

A perfect Mean Squared Error value is 0. This loss function is to be minimized and does not reflect whether the model over estimate or underestimate the target value. The Mean Squared Error function is typically used when the output values are continuous values or for linear regression. In artificial neural networks, the Mean Square Error may cause an issue of slow convergence if the Sigmoid function is used as activation function.

A variant of the Mean Square Error is the Mean Squared Logarithmic Error. What differentiate the Mean Squared Logarithmic Error from the Mean Square Error we just described is the application of a logarithm function on both the predicted value of the output Y_{pred} and the true value of the output Y_{act}. This function is given by the following equation: $L = (1/m) * (\sum [\log (Y_{ac} + 1) - \log (Y_{pred} + 1)]^2)$, with m number observations of outputs.

The Mean Squared Logarithmic Error does not penalize heavily when the residual of the actual value and the predicted value is very large. It penalizes more if the model is underestimating the target values than it is overestimating the target values. Generally, the Mean Squared Logarithmic Error is similar to the

Mean Square Error if the residual is small and if the residual between the actual value Y_{act} and the estimated value Y_{pred} is very large or one of the values either the estimated or the target value is large, the value of the Mean Squared Logarithmic Error is very small or negligible compared to the Mean Square Error.

Other loss functions used is machine learning and for neural networks is the norm L1 and the norm L2. The norm L1 simply the sum of the absolute value of the residuals between the predicted values of the output Y_{pred} and the actual true values of the output Y_{act}. The L1 norm loss function is given by the following equation: $L = \sum | Y_{act} - Y_{pred} |$. The L2 norm is similar to the L1 norm by summing the square of the residuals and similar to Mean Square Error without a division on the number of observations of the output m. Mathematically the L2 norm loss function is given by the equation: $L = \sum (Y_{act} - Y_{pred})^2$.

Mean Absolute Error is another loss function that has similar properties of the L1 norm function. It is computed as the sum of the absolute value of residuals between the target and predicted output values divided by the number of observations of the output. Mathematically the equation of the Mean Absolute Error is: $L = \sum | Y_{act} - Y_{pred} |^2$. These loss functions may seem similar however they have different properties.

For instance, the Mean Squared Error makes it easy to calculate the gradient unlike the Mean absolute Error. The L2 norm and Mean Squared Error penalizes heavily on the large values of the output especially when the residuals between the target and the predicted value is large.

The reason for this is that they apply a square to the residuals. In contrast, the L1 norm and the Mean Absolute Error are less sensitive to the large values because they do not use a square.

A variant of the Mean Absolute Error is the Mean Absolute Percentage Error. This loss function as it name suggest, provide the model error as percentage compared to the actual true value of the output. The Mean Absolute Percentage Error is given by the following equation:

$L = (1/m) * \sum | (Y_{act} - Y_{pred}) / Y_{act}| * 100$, with m is the number of observations of outputs. The Mean Absolute Percentage Error function cannot be used if the output values have zero values.

The reason for that is because we by the target actual value of the output Y_{act} and we cannot divide by 0. Another downside of the Mean Absolute Percentage Error is does not provide an upper bound for large values of overestimated target value. In fact, when the output values or the residual between the actual and the predicted output values is small, the Mean Absolute

Percentage Error is less than 100, but when the outputs are very large the value of the Absolute Percentage Error can exceed 100.

The Mean Absolute Percentage Error can be useful to compare between different models with different outputs because it provides a relative error. So far, we just presented loss functions that can be used for linear regression or when we are trying to optimize a variable that have continuous values. Next we will talk about loss functions that can be used when the variable is binary variable.

Another widely used loss function is the logistic loss or logarithm loss. The logistic loss is also called the Cross Entropy. This loss function is mainly used when the output values are binary (i.e. 0 or 1) or represents a probability. Estimated probabilities are compared to the target output value.

Then a score is computed according to the distance between the target value and the estimated value in order to penalize that probability. In fact, it applies a logarithmic penalty where small distance has a small score and the large distance are scored with high values. The logarithmic loss is to be minimized. Smaller values represent small model error and closer the value is to 0 the perfect the model is. Mathematically the Cross Entropy or the logistic loss function is defined by the equation: $L = - (1 / m)$

* $\sum$ [Y_{act} * log (Y_{pred}) + (1 -Y_{act}) * log (1 -1 Y_{pred})], where m is the number of observations of the outputs. The Cross Entropy can be used for classification in multi-classes. Another logarithmic type of loss function that can be used is the Negative Logarithmic Likelihood.

This loss function is similar to the logistic loss function and is computed as follows:

$L = - (1 / m) * \sum$ log (Y_{pred}). This function cannot really be used for the training a machine learning model. This function is rather used in artificial neural networks in order to measure the accuracy of a classifier model. The Negative Logarithmic Likelihood is only used when the model outputs are a probability for an input to belong to each class rather than just an estimate of the high likely class.

Another used loss function for classifier models is the Hinge loss function. This loss function is also called max-margin objective function. The hinge loss function is computed directly on the output of the model classification or probability not the class tag.

For a target actual output Y_{act} and the predicted value by the model Y_{pred}, the hinge loss function is as given by the following equation: $L = (1 / m) * \sum$ max (0, 1 - Y_{act} * Y_{pred}) where m is the number of observation of outputs. When both the actual and the predicted values are positive or negative (i.e. have the same sign) it means that the model predicts the accurate class. The hinge loss function is 0.

When the actual and the predicted output values have opposite signs, which means the model does not predict the right class, the hinge loss function is increasing. There is a more generalized formula of the hinge function that is given by the following equation: $L = (1 / m) * \sum \max (0, a - Y_{act} * Y_{pred})$ where a is a user defined value and m is the number of observation of outputs.

The hinge loss function has a variant function called the Squared Hinge loss function. This loss function applies a squared value to max-margin value. The squared Hinge loss function is given by the following equation: $L = (1 / m) * \sum (\max (0, a - Y_{act} * Y_{pred}))^2$.

To train a machine learning model or an artificial neural network, the loss function should be chosen according to the problem being solved. In this section we presented different loss functions that can be used. So, if the model or the artificial neural network is classifier, a logistic or a loss function that uses a logarithm should be used.

In contrast, if linear regression problem is being solved a loss function like the Mean square Error or norm L1 or L2 can be used. Keep in mind that some loss function penalizes heavily on large values like the L2 norm or the Mean Squared error. If we want to emphasize the small values, the Mean Squared Logarithmic Error is more suited than the other loss functions.

Feedforward and back propagation

The process of feedforward and back-propagation was proposed back in the 70s. Since then it is the most efficient and widely used process to train artificial neural networks. This process has proven its efficiency to solve non-linear ill-defined complex problems. So how does feedforward and back propagation work?

The feedforward is the first step to take. It consists of running the neural network using the training dataset as inputs. Basically, by feedforward we mean passing the training dataset and information through the network from the input layer to the output layer. In this process all neurons apply their calculation to convert the information and pass it the output layer as final prediction according to the input layer. Afterwards the loss function is calculated. We want the value of the loss function to be as close as possible to 0. In other words, we want the predicted output value to be as similar as possible to the target actual output value. After the evaluation of the loss function, its value is fed backwards within the neural network to adjust the weights.

The value of the loss function is processed back from the output layer to the neurons in the hidden layer connected to it and so on until the input layer. The loss function is propagated backwards as a signal where neuron captures just a fraction of that signal according to the contribution or impact (i.e. weight) has to compute the predicted output.

The process is applied to all layers in the network. After the back propagation, the weights of each neuron are adjusted according to loss function signal propagated. Typically, the weights are adjusted using a delta rule which is the loss function signal.

The weights are adjusted in small increments based on the gradients of the loss function. This technique is called the gradient descent. In this algorithm the gradient point towards the direction to follow to reach the global minimum of the loss function. We will explain in details the gradient descent algorithm in the next chapter when we will present the optimization algorithms.

To summarize the training process of an artificial neural network is an iterative process where the weights are adjusted using the training dataset. The process alternates between feedforward propagation and back propagation.

 The same training dataset is fed to neural network several times and the loss function is computed and back propagated and the weights are adjusted accordingly at each iteration until a satisfactory performance is achieved. In some cases, the neural network does not learn. Simply the algorithm does not converge and the loss function is very high. In other words, the predicted output by the neural network diverge greatly from the desired output values. The element that should be checked in these cases is the data. There are two scenarios that might explain the reason why the neural network is unable to learn from the data.

The first scenario is there insufficient information within the data or insufficient data feature that neural network can learn from to predict the output. The second scenario is that there is insufficient a mount of the data that will enable the neural network to learn from the data.

Hence a special attention should be given to the data in order to train an effective neural network. Overall, training an artificial neural network is an optimization problem that requires an objective function or loss function to optimize and an optimization algorithm to perform the optimization. In the next chapter we will go through some optimization algorithms that can be used to train an artificial neural network.

Chapter 4: Learning algorithms

So far, we have learnt the fundamentals of machine learning and artificial neural network. We also learnt the big picture of the process of training an artificial neural network. In this chapter we will go into the details of the training process of a machine learning model and artificial neural network.

In this chapter, we will present in details how the optimization algorithms work and how they are implemented for training machine learning models. But first let's define some terminology we will be using in this chapter. We are going to make first the difference between a parameter and a hyperparameter. A parameter is typically a configuration of the model that defines that distinguish the model from other models. The parameter can be approximated from the data. In artificial neural networks the weights are the parameters that makes each artificial neural network unique.

Hyperparameter, however, are the configurations that do not affect the model and does not define model. The hyperparameters are parameters or configurations that defined by the modeler to define and train the model or tune the learning algorithms. In an artificial neural network hyperparameters are for example the number of neurons, hidden layers, the algorithm optimizer and the number of iterations among others. The number of iterations is also called epoch and refers the number of times the artificial neural network has performed the feedforward and the back-propagation processes to learn.

The number of epochs should be increased until the evaluation criteria of the artificial neural tested on the validation dataset is decreasing. Now that we distinguish between parameters and hyperparameters, let's discover what algorithms we can use to train machine learning and artificial neural networks.

Optimization algorithms are simply algorithms that has the goal of optimizing (i.e. minimizing or maximizing) an objective function. There is a variety of optimization algorithms.

We cite the gradient descent algorithms, genetic algorithms, Newton method, Simulated Annealing, Evolutionary algorithms among others. In general, we can distinguish zero order algorithms, first order algorithms and second order algorithms.

The zero-order algorithms are algorithms that are also called derivative free and do not use any form of the derivatives of the loss function. These algorithms are used when the derivative of the loss function is very complex to obtain.

The first order algorithms typically use the gradient of the first derivative of the loss function and the second order algorithms use the second derivative of the loss function. The derivatives are computed in respect to the parameters.

The widely used algorithm in machine learning is the gradient descent algorithm which belongs to the first-order algorithm category.

There is some variation of this algorithm. In this chapter, we will go into details of applying the gradient descent algorithm as well as some of its variations.

4.1 _Gradient descent algorithm_

The gradient descent is one the most widely used algorithm in machine learning for its efficiency and is very straightforward. The gradient descent algorithm as its name indicate is based on the gradient of the loss function. In other words, it is based on the first derivative of function. Remember that the first derivative is null that means it is a minimum value.

Therefore, the gradient descent updates the weight parameter based on the gradient of the function at each layer starting from the output layer to the input layer. That is the specific reason why activation functions must have a derivative or gradient defined in order to apply the gradient descent.

So, the gradient points toward which direction to follow in order to minimize the loss the function. Typically, the parameters are updated according to the negative value of the gradient. The value of the gradient is factorized by a parameter called the learning rate. At each iteration the weights are updated until the minimum is reached.

The learning rate will dictate how fast we reach that minimum. Now let's see how we would apply this algorithm on a linear regression. Remember that in linear regression we are trying to approximate a function f such as $f(X) = W * X + b$ where W is the weights and b is the bias. Let's assume the L is a loss function that we are trying to optimize. Typically, the function L is something like $L = (1/m) * \sum (y_{predicted} - y_{target})^2$ where $y_{predicted}$ is estimated by the model and y_{target} is the target value. The loss function we described here is the Root Mean Square Error know as the RMSE and is widely used in optimization. The loss function L can be written as:

$L = (1/m) * \sum [(W * X+B) - y_{target}]^2$. We just replaced $y_{predicted}$ by the its value computed by the function f we are trying to estimate. So, first let's describe the steps of the gradient descent and then we will go into details of each step. Let's assume that we have pre-defined learning rate parameter α and a number of maximum iterations or epochs N fixed.

The algorithm steps are summarized as follows: 1) it starts by assigning random values to the weights W and the bias b, 2) the algorithm runs the model W and b, 3) the algorithm evaluate the loss function, 4) the algorithm calculate the value of the partial derivatives $\delta L / \delta W$ and $\delta L / \delta B$, 5) the algorithm updates the weights as follows: $W = W - \alpha * (\delta L / \delta W)$ and the bias as : $B = B - \alpha * (\delta L / \delta B)$, then it goes backs to step number until the loss function does no longer improve or the maximum number of iterations is reached.

Now you can see from the steps of the gradient descent, we have some hyper-parameters to define in order to apply the algorithm for a learning process. The first hyper-parameter is the learning rate parameter α. The learning rate should be chosen carefully because if it is fixed into a large value the algorithm may never converge. The reason for that is that the algorithm might miss the minimum. In contrast if the learning parameter is fixed into a small value, the algorithm will converge very slowly and then be very computationally inefficient.

To get a better understanding of the impact of the learning rate on the convergence of the gradient descent algorithm, let's take an explicit example. Say we have a gradient or a first derivative of a Loss function of value 2.3 and the α learning parameter rate is 0.1. Then parameter will be updated or more specifically decreased by 0.23. If the learning parameter was 0.01 instead of 0.1, then parameter will be decreased by 0.023. Typically, the learning parameter is fixed in a value ranging from 0.001 to 0.3. In case the algorithm does not converge and the learning process in successful, it is recommended to test smaller learning parameter values. To train an artificial neural network using the gradient descent algorithm, we apply the same the steps. In step 3 the weights are updated for each layer by computing the gradient for the activation function of each layer starting from the output layer to the input layer as we explained in the previous chapter during the back-propagation process.

The initialization of the weights is very important in an artificial neural network training using the gradient descent algorithm. The reason for that is the neuron has similar weights then they will have the similar gradient. Hence these neurons will catch the same characteristics in the learning process. Therefore, it is recommended to initialize the weights randomly.

The gradient descent is a deterministic algorithm meaning applying the algorithm over and over with a fixed hyper-parameter will provide the same results. The algorithm is applied on the whole training dataset and uses a fixed learning rate. Another better way to it is adjusting the learning rate parameter by decreasing its value when we approach the maximum of epoch or simply when we approach a solution.

Therefore, we can use an additional hyper-parameter which is called the learning rate decay. This parameter allows adjusting the learning parameter. When the algorithm is at the very beginning of the learning process the values of the learning parameter are very high to allow for bigger steps to update the weights.

As the learning process goes forward, the learning rate is decreasing in order to convergence to the minimum value or the optimal value of the loss function. Now that you understand the general concept of the gradient descent algorithm, let's discover the variations of this algorithm which are the stochastic gradient descent, the batch gradient descent and the mini-batch gradient descent.

4.2 *Stochastic, batch and mini batch gradient descent*

First of all, is worth mentioning that all variations of the gradient descent algorithm follow the same steps we described in the previous sections. The only difference is at what frequency they compute the gradient and update the parameters and the quantity of data used to update the parameters.

The stochastic gradient descent is the variation of the gradient descent that updates the parameters more frequently. It actually updates the parameters for each entry of the training dataset. In other words, if we have N observation in the training dataset, each observation is fed at a time and processed through the whole neural network.

The weights are updated accordingly for each observation of the training dataset at a time. This version has some advantages and disadvantages. The good side of the stochastic gradient is that it might converge quickly in some cases and is less prone to get stuck into a local minimum. However, it may become computationally expensive because it uses one observation from the training dataset at a time to update the parameters.

Also, this algorithm does not take advantage of fast computation of vectorization of matrix form. The batch gradient descent uses the contradictory concept of the stochastic gradient descent algorithm. Instead of updating the weights and the bias parameters after each observation is processed, the weights are updated after all observations are processed through the neural network or through the model.

Therefore, at each iteration the whole training dataset is process through the model and the weights are updated once the loss function and the gradient are evaluated for the whole training dataset. The downside of the batch gradient descent algorithms is it is high likely to get stuck in a local minimum. This algorithm can also cause memory problems in order to handle large datasets in one single shot unlike the stochastic gradient descent.

However, this algorithm provides a steady gradient descent unlike the stochastic gradient descent. The third variation of the gradient descent which is the mini batch gradient descent is a hybrid gradient descent that combines both stochastic and gradient descent algorithms.

The mini batch gradient descent is developed to overcome the drawbacks of both stochastic and the batch gradient descent algorithms which are large memory requirements, computational efficiency, take advantage of vectorization and matrix forms as well as avoiding getting trapped in a local minimum.

So, the concept of the mini batch is basically dividing the training dataset into smaller groups with equal size. Each group is called a batch. The same principle of the batch gradient descent is applied into each batch of the training dataset. Let's say for example we a training dataset of N observations. Then the training dataset is subdivided into 5 batches where each batch contain N/5 observations or samples. Then we iterate the gradient descent on the five batches.

Note in this section we talked about the fact the gradient descent is prone to get trapped in a local minimum. This typically happens when the loss function is a non-convex function. The non-convex functions have several local minimums.

The goal of optimization is finding the global minimum or an its approximation. In order to avoid getting trapped in a local minimum, we can repeat the learning process with the gradient descent by choosing a different random initial weights and bias. We can also use a hyper-parameter called momentum can be used.

The momentum is a parameter that is fixed to a value between 0 and 1. It has role of weighting the average of the gradient that was previously computed in order to define the step applied to update the parameters. In other words, the momentum is a fraction of the past update of the parameters that is added to the current update of the parameters. So, the parameters are updated as follow considering that the momentum hyper-parameter is denoted as δ:

$W_t = W_t - [\delta * W_{t-1} + \alpha * (\delta L / \delta W)]$ and the bias as:

$B_t = B_t - [\delta * B_{t-1} + \alpha * (\delta L / \delta B)]$.

To summarize implementing any variant of the gradient descent algorithm comes with some challenges. We have seen the algorithm can be trapped in a local minimum. To avoid that we can use the momentum hyper-parameter. The convergence of the algorithm is highly sensitive to the learning rate parameter.

An additional challenge is that the learning rate is fixed for all model parameters. Let's say for example we have a sparse data or sparse neurons due to an activation function. Remember sparsity is desirable characteristic in artificial neural network in order to avoid having a dense network. In this case, we would want to update the weights at different learning rates where the less frequent occurring features are less frequently updated.

To do so, we can use the Adaptive gradient algorithm within the gradient descent algorithm. The Adaptive gradient algorithm (Adagrad) is an algorithm that adjusts the learning rate according to the parameters by updating parameters of the less frequent occurring features with a high learning rate and the parameters of the frequent occurring features with a small learning rate.

The Adaptive gradient algorithm improves the performance of the gradient descent algorithm. The advantage of using this algorithm is that adjusting the learning rate manually by trying different values is no longer needed and is done automatically. Formally, the algorithm adapts each parameter using a different learning rate as follows: $W_{t+1} = W_t - dL * [\alpha / $ square root of (DL + ε)] and $B_{t+1} = B_t - dL * [\alpha / $ square root of (DL + ε)] where dL is derivative and DL is the sum of the derivatives of previous iteration with respect to all parameters. The downside of this algorithm is that over the iterations the learning rate α becomes smaller and smaller as the denominator is increasing by adding up the sum of the previous gradients. This problem is called the diminishing learning rate. This issue causes that algorithm stops learning. Adadelta is a variant of the Adaptive gradient algorithm that tries to resolve this issue.

The learning rate in the Adadelta algorithm is monotonically reduced. In fact, the Adadelta algorithm considers only a restricted window of size N of previous gradients when updating the parameters. The value of the current gradient is also included to calculation of the fraction by which the parameter is updated. If θ are the parameters for examples we try to estimate they are updated as follows: $\theta_{t+1} = \theta_t + D\theta_t$ where $D\theta_t = -[$ RMS$(D\theta_{t-1})$ / RMS$(DL)] * DL$ where DL is the gradient and $D\theta_t$ is the gradient with respect to the parameter θ at time step t.

4.3 _Adam algorithm_

The Adam algorithm is a recent algorithm developed specifically to train artificial neural networks. Specifically, the Adam algorithm was introduced by two researchers Diederik Kingma and Jimmy Ba in 2015 through a poster entitled Adm: A method for stochastic Optimization '. The name of the algorithm originates from Adaptive Moment estimation.

It started to gain some popularity in machine learning and has proven efficiency in some studies over the gradient descent algorithm. The authors of this algorithm claim that implementing the Adam algorithm for non-convex optimization like training artificial neural networks has some benefits.

These benefits include that the algorithm is simple to use, is computationally efficient, does not require large memory, the algorithm is adapted support handling large dataset or optimizing multiple parameters, is suited for non-stationary objectives and for solving problems with objective function having noisy gradient or sparse gradient as well as the little requirements to adjust the hyper-parameters. The Adam algorithm is still in continuous improvement and update. In this section we will go through the basics of this algorithm.

The Adam algorithm uses some similarities of the stochastic gradient algorithm with a momentum parameter included. In fact, the Adam algorithm adapts the learning rate parameter according to the parameters. In other words, the algorithm adjusts different learning rates for the parameters of the model.

The Adam algorithm uses both the first and second moment of the gradient in order to adjust the learning rates. In fact, the Adam algorithm, as introduced by its authors, is developed to take advantage of two algorithms the Adaptive Gradient Algorithm as well as Root Mean Square propagation. The adaptive gradient algorithm adjusts the parameters according to the frequency or occurrence of feature. Hence it considers the sparsity of data.

The Root Mean Square Propagation is the part of the Adam that considers the momentum hyper-parameter by adjusting the parameters according to their change in the previous iteration. The particularity of the Adam algorithm is that uses the uncentred second moment or the uncentred variance instead of the first moment which is the average used the gradient descent when the momentum hyper-parameter is used. By uncentred second moment means that the mean is not subtracted when computing the second moment which is the variance.

The Adam algorithm use the squared gradient in order to compute the decay learning rate as a function of the decay learning rate of the previous iteration as follows:
$m_t = \beta_1 * m_{t-1} + (1 - \beta_1) * DL$; $v_t = \beta_2 * v_{t-1} + (1 - \beta_2) * |DL|^2$;
where m_t is an estimate of the mean of the gradient and v_t is an estimate of the uncentered variance of the gradient. The parameters β_1 and β_2 are the learning rates decay and DL is the gradient. The two estimates of the mean and the uncentred variance are initialized to null. To update the parameters, they apply the following equation: $W_{t+1} = W_t - [\alpha * M_t / (\text{square root} (V_t) + \varepsilon]$ and the bias as:

$B_{t+1} = B_t - [\alpha * M_t / (\text{square root } (V_t) + \varepsilon]$; where $M_t = m_t / (1 - \beta_{1,t})$ and $V_t = v_t / (1 - \beta_{2,t})$. The parameters M_t and V_t are a biased correction of the two estimates of the mean and the variance m_t and v_t of the gradient. The recommended default values of the $\beta 1$ and $\beta 2$ by the authors is 0.9.

Regarding the parameter ε the recommended default value is 10^{-8}. As for the gradient descent algorithm, Adam algorithm has some variants to resolve some its issues. We cite the Adamax and Nadam algorithms. We will go in details of these algorithms in the next section.

4.4 Adamax and Nadam

Adam algorithm uses the L^2 norm of the previous gradients to update the parameters. Adamax simply uses L^∞ norm instead of the L^2 to update the parameters. This norm allows to provide stable results.

So, the estimates of the variance become: $v_t = \beta 2 * v_{t-1} + (1 - \beta 2) * |DL|^\infty = \max (\beta 2 * v_{t-1}, |DL|)$ instead of $v_t = \beta 2 * v_{t-1} + (1 - \beta 1) * |DL|^2$. Now the parameters are updated as: $W_{t+1} = W_t - [\alpha * M_t / V_t]$ and the bias as: $B_{t+1} = B_t - [\alpha * M_t / V_t]$. Here the v_t is based on the maximum function so it is not subject to bias toward 0.

Therefore, a bias correction is not required for v_t. The recommended values of the hyper-parameters $\beta 1$ and $\beta 2$ is 0.9 and 0.99 resp. and 0.002 for the α parameter.

Nadam is another variant of the Adam algorithm that combines Adam algorithm with the Nesterov-accelerated gradient. The Nesterov accelerated gradient is another variant that belongs to the adaptive learning rate algorithms.

 This algorithm computes the derivative with respect to the following step instead of the current step. So, the updated value of a parameter θ is as follows: $\theta = \theta - v_t$ where $v_t = \delta * v_{t-1} + \alpha *$ DL $(\theta - \delta * v_{t-1})$ and $\theta - \delta * v_{t-1}$ is the gradient according to the following step. The Nesterov accelerated gradient is an improvement of the momentum. So, the Nadam algorithm uses the concept of the Nestroc accelerated gradient within the Adam paradigm. The Nadam is mainly used when the derivative is noisy or if the derivative has high deviation. In the Nadam algorithm the learning process is rushed by the sum of the exponential of the decay learning of the average of the previous and the current derivative.

4.5 *How to choose an algorithm*

In this chapter, we have seen that there are different variants of the gradient descent algorithms. So now you are wondering how to choose a variant to implement. One single rule can be applied is that if the data present some sparsity, then it is better suited to implement some adaptive learning algorithm whether it is the Adam algorithm or the gradient descent with an extension as the Adaptive gradient algorithm.

The advantage of these algorithms is they don't require adjusting the learning rate manually. Also, with these algorithms it is high likely to reach performant results just with default values of the hyper-parameters. Although the computational efficiency of the Adam algorithm, some studies showed that the Adam algorithm is not adapted for some domains and may not converge into optimal results.

In general research has so far showed that for model that solve problems like image recognition or classification, they are better trained using the gradient descent algorithm with momentum. However, if a problem is complex and is solved by a deep neural network, it best suited to use an adaptive learning rate algorithm like Adam or the Adaptive gradient learning.

Conclusion

Thank you for making it through to the end of Machine learning for beginners: step-by-step guide to learning and mastering machine learning for absolute beginners, let's hope it was informative and able to provide you with all of the tools you need to achieve your goals whatever they may be.

The objective of this book is to provide a beginning guide for the absolute beginners with no prior knowledge in machine learning and want an introduction of the general concepts of machine learning and artificial neural networks. This book does not require any pre-requisite skills to understand and follow the concepts presented.

The book covers the concept of machine learning, the types of machine learning namely supervised, unsupervised, semi-supervised and reinforcement learning. It also covers the basics of artificial neural networks, activation functions, the types of artificial neural networks including the perceptron, the feedforward neural networks, recurrent neural networks, convolutional neural networks and the modular neural networks.

The book presents how the artificial neural networks as well as the loss function that can be used depending on the problem that is being solved by the artificial neural network. Finally, the book presents the widely used algorithm for training artificial neural networks as well any machine learning model the gradient descent as well as its variants the stochastic gradient descent, batch gradient descent and the mini-batch gradient.

Machine learning and artificial neural networks are an active research field. Research is interest in improving the machine learning paradigms, the structure of artificial neural as well as optimal methods for training machine learning model and artificial neural networks.

The reason for that is that machine learning is black art where there is no clear guidance on how to apply it. Apply a machine learning model or an artificial neural network requires a trial and error procedure in order to find the optimal settings. The success of implementing whether a machine learning model or an artificial neural network depends on the success of the trial and error procedure as well as the experience of the modeler to make decisions regarding the model settings.

Once you have acquired the knowledge and the skills presented in this book, you should be able to make a clear judgment on which strategy and model type you should choose to solve a specific problem with machine learning.

Finally, if you found this book useful in any way, a review on Amazon is always appreciated!

Machine Learning With Python:

The Ultimate Guide for Absolute Beginners with Steps to Implement Artificial Neural Networks with Real Examples (Useful Python Tools eg. Anaconda, Jupiter Notebook)

By

Daniel Géron

Introduction

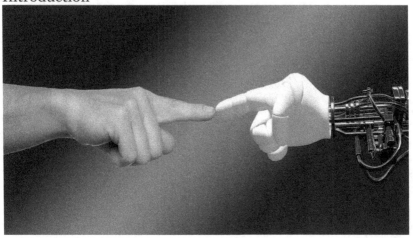

Congratulations for buying *Machine Learning With Python* and thank you for doing so.

This book is intended to be an initiation to learn machine learning with Python programming for absolute beginners that have no background in programming. It provides the basics of both machine learning and Python programming. It also provides a guide to use Python libraries to build machine learning models.

This book has mainly four chapters that will help you understand models of machine learning and to how to carry them out in a Python environment. Chapters 1 and 2 are dedicated to machine learning principles, the third chapter for

Python programming and its basic syntax. Finally, the four chapters provide applications of machine learning with Python.

The first chapter discusses the fundamentals and concepts of machine learning. You will learn the different learning machine paradigms, namely supervised, unsupervised, and reinforcement paradigms. Basically, this chapter helps enhance understanding the different paradigms of machine learning, the cases when each paradigm is applied. This chapter also explains some widely used algorithms in machine learning and the process to create a model of machine learning.

In the second chapter, we will discuss the artificial neural networks, a tool widely used in machine learning. Because, the artificial neural network is a machine learning branch by itself, it is best covered in a separate chapter. You will learn the principle of neural networks, types of neural networks, and how to train these neural networks. This chapter explains in detail the different components of an artificial neural network.

In the third chapter, you will tackle Python programming. You will learn why Python is useful to develop machine learning models. You will also learn how to get started with Python, running Python programs, and basic syntax of Python programming. You will also explore some useful platforms that use Python if you prefer using a graphical user interface instead of a command line.

In chapter four, you learn how to apply machine learning with Python. This chapter contains some machine learning applications that were discussed in the previous chapters. You will get through detailed examples in order to run machine learning models using Python tools you learned in chapter 3. The examples cover the paradigms of machine learning and steps to develop a multilayer neural network without relying on the pre-coded functions in Python as well as using the built-in function of Python libraries. Through these examples, you will apply Python skills to process and analyze and visualize the dataset.

Several books discussing this particular subject exist on the market. Thanks for deciding to read this book. To ensure the book covers the most relevant information for a beginner, a lot of effort was taken. Enjoy reading and learning!

Chapter 1: The Concept of Machine Learning

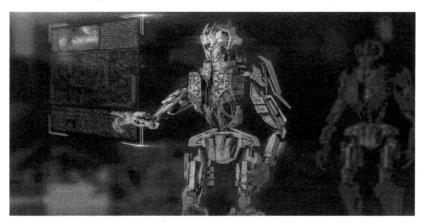

Derived from Artificial Intelligence, the concept of machine learning is a complete area of study. It focusses on developing automated programs to acquire knowledge from data in order to make a diagnosis or a prediction. Machine learning relies on the concept that machines are able to learn, identify trends, and provide decisions with minimal human intervention. These machines improve with experience and build the principals that govern the learning processes.

There is a wide variety of machine learning uses, such as marketing, speech and image recognition, smart robots, web search, etc. Machine learning requires large dataset in order to train the model and get accurate predictions. Different types of machine learning exist and can typically be classified into two separate categories supervised or unsupervised learning. Other algorithms can be labeled as semi-supervised learning or reinforcement machine learning.

Supervised learning is mainly used to learn from a categorized or labeled dataset than applied to predict the label for the unknown dataset. In contrast, unsupervised learning is used when the training dataset is neither categorized nor labeled and is applied to study how a function can describe a hidden pattern from the dataset. Semi-supervised learning uses together categorized and non-categorized dataset. Reinforcement is a method that relies on the trial and error process to identify the most accurate behavior in an environment to improve its performance.

This chapter will go through the details for each type of machine learning and explains in-depth the differences between each type of learning and their pros and cons. Let's start with the supervised learning that is commonly used and the simplest learning paradigm in machine learning. Before we dive into the details about machine learning when machine learning is the best approach to solve a problem?

When is best to use machine learning?

It is crucial to understand machine learning is not the go-to approach to solve any problem in hand. Some problematics can be solved with robust approaches without relying on machine learning. Problematics with few data with target value that can easily be defined by a deterministic approach. In this case, when it is easy to determine and program a rule that drives the target value, machine learning is not the best approach to follow. Machine learning is best used when it is impossible to develop and code a rule to define the target value. For instance, image and speech recognition is a perfect example of when machine learning is best used. Images, for example, has a lot of features and pixels that a simple human task are very hard to implement in order to recognize the image. A human being can visually recognize an image and classify it. But how to develop an algorithm and a rule-based approach is exhausting and not very effective for image recognition. So, in this case building an image dataset and flag each image with its specific contents (i.e., animal, flower, object, etc..) and use a machine learning algorithm to detect each category of images is very efficient. In short, machine learning is very handy when you have a number of factors that impacts the target value with little correlation.

Machine learning is also the best approach to automate a task for large datasets. For example, it is easy to detect manually a spam email or a fraudulent transaction. However, it is very time consuming and tedious tasks to the same task for a hundred million emails or transaction. Machine learning is very cost effective and computationally efficient to handle large datasets and large-scale problems.

Machine learning is also best used in cases where human expertise to solve a problem is very limited. An example of these problems is when it is impossible to label or categorize the data. Machine learning in this situation is used to learn from the datasets and provide answers for the problems or the questions we are trying to solve.

Overall, machine learning is best used to solve problem when: 1) human have the expertise to solve the problem but it almost impossible to develop easily a program to mimic the human task, 2) human have no expertise or an idea regarding the target value (i.e., no label or classified data), 3) human have the expertise and knows the possible target values but it has cost-effective and time consuming to implement such an approach. In general machine learning is best used to solve complex data-driven problems like learning behaviors for clients targeting or acquisition, fraud analysis, anomaly detection in large systems, diseases diagnostic, shape/image and speech recognition among others. Problems when few data are available, and human expertise can be easily programmed as rule-based approach it is best to use a deterministic rule-based method to resolve the problem. The large dataset should be available so as machine learning to be efficient and effective — otherwise, issues of generality and overfitting rise. Generality means the ability of a model to be applied in case scenarios similar to case scenarios that served to build the model. When machine learning models are built on a small dataset, they become very inefficient when applied on new datasets that they have not been exposed to. Hence, their applicability becomes very limited. For example, building a model that recognizes an image as a cat or dog image, then apply the same with new images data of other animals. The model will give an inaccurate classification of the new dataset of the other animals like dog or cat image. Overfitting is when the model shows a high accuracy when applied on the training data, and its accuracy drops drastically when applied to a test data similar to the training data. Another issue with machine learning that should be considered in developing a machine learning model is the similarity between inputs which are associated with several outputs. It becomes very difficult to apply a classification machine learning model in this case as similar inputs yield to different outputs. Therefore, the quality and quantity of data are very important in machine learning. One should keep in mind that not only the quantity of data but also the quality of data affects the accuracy and applicability of any machine learning approach. If the right data is not available, collecting the right data is crucial and is the first step to take in order to adopt a machine learning approach. Now, you have learned when it is useful to adopt a machine learning approach, when you should avoid machine learning and when a simple rule-based deterministic approach is the simple way to solve a problem. Next, you will learn the different types of machine learning that you might use when each type is applied, the data that it requires, widely used algorithms and the steps to follow to solve a problem with machine learning.

What is supervised learning?

In supervised learning, we typically have a training data set with corresponding labels. From the relationship that associates the training set and the labels, we try to label new unknown data sets. To do so, the learning algorithm is supplied with the training set and the corresponding correct labels. Then, it learns the relationship between the training set and the labels. That relationship is then applied by the algorithm to label the unknown data set. Formally, we want to build a model that estimates a function f that relates a data set X (i.e., input) to labels Y (i.e., output): $Y=f(X)$. The mathematical relationship f is called the mapping function.

Let's consider we have an ensemble of images and try to label it as a cat image or not cat. We first provide as an input to the learning algorithm images (X) and labels of these images (cat or not cat). Then, we approximate the relationship f that estimates Y according to X as accurately as possible: $Y=f(X)+\varepsilon$, ε is an error which is random with a mean zero. Note that we are approximating the relationship between the dataset and the labels and we want the error ε as close as possible to 0. When ε is exactly 0, that means the model is perfect and 100% accurate, which is very rare to build such a model.

Typically, a subset of available labeled data, which is often 80%, is utilized as a training set to estimate the mapping task to build such a model. The extra 20% of the labeled data is utilized to assess the model's efficiency and precision. At this step, the model is fed with the 20% data, and the predicted output is compared to the actual labels to compute the model performance.

Supervised learning has mainly two functions, namely, *classification* or *regression*. Classification is used when the output Y is a quality or category data (i.e., discrete variable) whereas regression is used when the output Y is quantity data (i.e., continuous numerical values). Classification aims at predicting a label or assigning data to a class to which they are most similar. The output Y is a binary variable (i.e., 0 or 1). The example is given above, labeling images as cat or no cat is an example of classification. The model can also be a multi-class classification where the model predicts different classes. For example, Outlook classifies mails in more than a category like Focused, Other, Spam. There are a number of algorithms that can be used, such as logistic regression, decision tree, random forest, multilayer perceptron. Regression is used when we want to predict a value such as a house pricing, human height, or weight. Linear regression is the simplest model for this type of problems.

The disadvantage of supervised learning is the fact that they cannot process new information, and training should be reconsidered when new information is available. For instance, we have a set of training images of dogs and cats, and the model is trained to label images as dog image or cat image. In other words, we have developed a model with two categories of dogs and cats. When this model is presented with new images of other animals, for example, a tiger, it labels incorrectly the tiger image as a dog or cat image. The model does not recognize the tiger image, but it provides a classification of the image in a category. Therefore, the model should be trained whenever new information is available.

In the next sub-sections, we cover the most commonly used algorithms to solve regression and a classification problem.

Linear Regression is a model typically used, as mentioned before, for supervised learning with a regression type problematic where the output is a continuous variable. Linear regression describes the relationship between an independent variable or multiple variables X and a target output variable Y:

Y=WX+B.

If X is a single variable, then W and B are constant parameters to be determined. Otherwise, W is a matrix, and B is the vector to be determined if we are dealing with multiple input variables. W is called the coefficients or weights of X, and B is called the intercept or Bias.

In the training process, we try to find the best parameters W and B that provides a predicted value of Y that are as similar to the actual values of Y. Then, optimal W and B are used to predict Y values from the input X. In this case, how do we know what values are optimum for B and W?

To identify the best parameters, i.e., weight W and bias B, we use what is called a cost or loss function J. A cost function quantifies how close the predicted value is to the target value of Y. Basically, this function quantifies the model error between the estimated and targeted values of Y. This function is to be minimized by the learning algorithm. Mathematically the cost function is:

$$\text{Loss function} = (1/m) * \sum (y_{predicted} - y_{target})^2$$

The cost function here is the Root Mean Squared Error, abbreviated RMSE, between the model's projected value and the target actual value of Y. Here, we are using the least square technique to approximate W and B's optimum values.

We can use an optimization algorithm like the *Gradient Descent* algorithm by updating intercept B and coefficient W values in such a way that it minimizes the value of the cost function. This algorithm starts with random values of W and B and updates these values at each iteration until it reaches a minimal value of the cost function J as follows:

$$W = W - \alpha * (\delta J / \delta W)$$
$$B = B - \alpha * (\delta J / \delta B)$$

Where α is a learning rate parameter, δJ is the derivative of the cost or loss function. We will learn the importance of the gradient of the cost function in the neural network section. The learning rate α is a parameter that determines how fast the algorithm learns. If the learning rate parameter has a low value, the slower the Weights and the bias parameters are updated. The algorithm will then converge very slowly. On the contrary, if the learning rate parameter has a high value, the faster the algorithm converges.

Here we presented a simple example of a linear regression model. Depending on the data, the relationship may not be linear. In this case, a non-linear regression model should be considered using the same principle.

Logistic regression is a classification method when the output is a discrete or binary variable (i.e., 0 or 1 / yes or no). Logistic regression has the same concept as the linear regression with the exception that it uses a logistic function or sigmoid function as a cost function and is based on probabilities. The logistic function is mathematically formulated as the equation given below:

$$F(X)=L/(1+\exp(-X))$$

The Sigmoid function is a logistic function where L is equal to 1. This function takes values between 0 and 1. It converts any value into ranges between 0 and, which is very useful in machine learning to map probabilities of input to belong to a specific class. Let's consider the example of classifying images as cat image or non-cat image. Basically, when using a Sigmoid function, we set a threshold value to discriminate between a cat image or non-cat image. The image is classified in cat image or not if the predicted value is greater or not than the fixed threshold.

In order to get values between 0 and 1, we apply the following transformation to the input X:

$$Z=B_0+B_1X$$

The regression is applied to the new variable Z. The cost function for a logistic regression is given then as follows:

Cost function$=-\log\{1/[1+\exp(-Z)]\}$ if the target value y is equal to 1

Cost function$=-\log\{1-1/[1+\exp(-Z)]\}$ if the target value y is equal to 0

We can express the two equations into one compressed equation as follows:

Cost function$=-1/n\sum[y\log(h(Z)) + (1-y)\log(1-h(Z))]$
where $h(X)=1/(1+\exp(-X)$

Like the linear regression, an optimizer algorithm like the gradient descent can be applied to minimize the cost function.

What is unsupervised learning?

The Unsupervised paradigm learning is applied to determine the data's masked structure pattern in order to learn more from the data. In contrast with supervised learning, there is neither a correct answer or a training dataset to learn from. In this case, only input dataset X is available. The algorithms are used to identify the patterns in data without explicitly providing them with many information other than the data itself. In short, no guidance is provided to the algorithm to learn from the data. The algorithm relies on similarities, patterns, and differences to learn from the data. There are different types of unsupervised learning, namely *clustering, association,* and *anomaly detection.*

Clustering algorithms are applied to identify the inherent groupings in data. For instance, grouping patients by eating habits. Basically, clustering is ordering the unlabeled data into clusters. A cluster is an ensemble of data that are similar. Association is a learning method by a rule to be identified. This rule shows trends in the dataset; for example, patients with diabetes tend to have hypertension. The association describes patterns that occur together in a dataset. Anomaly detection, as its name suggests, it detects unusual data points within the dataset. This learning is practical to detect suspicious transactions or email, fraud detection, or errors within a system, among others. Overall, unsupervised learning is very useful for regression application where the expected output is completely unknown. This paradigm of learning provides valuable information about the data structure and patterns with no information supplied. We will cover, in this section, the major unsupervised learning algorithms.

Clustering models rely typically on similarity measures defined as a Probabilistic or a Euclidean distance. Different algorithms are available for clustering such as *K-means clustering, hidden Markov models, self-organizing maps, Gaussian mixture models,* and *Hierarchical clustering,* among others.

A widely used algorithm for unsupervised learning is *K-means clustering.* It belongs to the partitional category of algorithms that defines all clusters at once. The k-means algorithm groups similar data into a fixed number K of clusters according to their centroid (i.e., center). The cluster number k is a user-fixed parameter. The k-means algorithm determines a k number of centroids of each cluster and then associates data to the nearest cluster using the similarity measure. More precisely, the algorithm starts by forming an initial K centroid defined from a random selection of data. Every point of the dataset is allocated to the nearest center or centroid. Then, the centroids are recalculated for each cluster. This procedure is replicated several times as long as a convergence criterion has not been satisfied. The convergence criterion can be a very minimal change of the average data forming a cluster (i.e., centroids), or a minimal change of re-allocation of data to the clusters, or the maximum number of iterations has attained.

This algorithm is mainly used because it is simple to understand, and its implementation is very straightforward. It is also computationally efficient. However, there are some downsides to this algorithm. It is only applicable if the mean is defined. In other words, it is applicable only for continuous data. For example, if the data is binary or categorial, another function representing the center should be used like the k-mode, which provides values frequency. This algorithm is sensitive to data and outliers because it is based on the mean to define the centroid. A slight change in data or if data contains an outlier, it leads to high variations. Another issue with the k-means algorithms is it can be inefficient when clusters do not have a rounded shape because it uses a distance to the centroid of a cluster to assign each point of the data to a certain class. This algorithm is also deterministic in the sense that each point fit in only one class. In reality, clusters may be overlapping, and the k-means algorithm is not able to define overlapping clusters.

Hierarchical clustering, unlike the k-means clustering, defines clusters from pre-determined clusters. Depending on how algorithms define these clusters, two varieties of hierarchical clustering algorithms can be identified the *agglomerative* and *divisive* algorithms. The first type of hierarchical algorithms starts typically with each data point as an individual cluster. Then merge similar clusters iteratively into larger clusters until one cluster is formed. In contrast, divisive algorithms start with all data points as a single cluster called the root cluster than divide it iteratively into smaller clusters called child clusters. The divisive algorithms stop when every data point defines a separate cluster or what is called in singleton clusters. The hierarchical clustering suffers from the same drawback as the k-means clustering, which is its inability to define overlapping clusters.

Gaussian mixture models are a probabilistic approach that allows overcoming some of the issues faced with the clustering algorithms. With the Gaussian mixture models, every cluster is described by its centroid (i.e., mean), covariance and its size or weight. Basically, Gaussian mixture models categorize data based on their distribution.

Self-organizing maps are a very different approach than approaches described previously. Self-organizing maps are a category of artificial neural network that aims at decreasing the size of the input space. It is trained to provide a discretized description of the input space using competitive learning and neighborhood function to preserve the form of the data which is fed to the model. This category of the artificial neural network is completely different than the one cover in the next chapter. The later uses a correction learning paradigm to improve its prediction like backpropagation and gradient descent.

Association, another unsupervised learning technic, aim at identifying data features that frequently occur together, and data features that are correlated. It helps answer the question of what the value of a data feature can tell about another feature. The directionality in the association is very important. If a data feature A shows a specific trend about another feature B it does not necessarily mean that the feature B will show a trend for the feature A. For example, if clients that buy a product A tends to buy a product B that does not mean necessarily that clients that buy the product B tends to buy the product A. The association rule algorithm uses different measures to evaluate performance of the rule: 1) support,2) confidence and ,3) lift. In order to explain these evaluation metrics, let's take, for example, two features A and B for which we want to identify the hidden relationship. The support is expressed as the frequency (percentage) of events where A and B occur together. It can be calculated as the fraction of events when A and B occur together. Confidence is computed as the fraction of events including the feature B to the number of events containing the feature A. The lift is computed as the fraction of the confidence and support. If the lift is greater than 1, the features A and B are positively correlated. If the lift is less than 1, the features A and B are negatively correlated. If the lift is equal to 1, then the features, A and B are not correlated.

Overall, association rule algorithms are based on the frequency of occurrences across a dataset. The purpose is to detect association that occurs more frequently within the dataset than in a given random sampling. This approach is widely used in bioinformatics and basket data analysis. The later provides retailers with valuable information about items that clients tend to buy together.

Anomaly detection is also called outlier detection. Outliers are simply the points or members of a dataset that shows a different behavior or have a different pattern than the majority of the dataset members. These outliers can be identified visualizing by plotting the data. Sometimes the outliers are just an error in the dataset. For example, an error in measurements or human error in typing information in the system. These outliers can be removed from the dataset to be analyzed. In some cases, these outliers may contain valuable information rather than just a simple error, for example, fraudulent transactions or email spams, or detecting malignant tumors. In this case, we want to understand the outlier behaviors to prevent them in the future and to build a more robust model.

Anomaly detection can be either point, contextual, or collective. The first anomaly, point anomaly, is simply a point of a dataset that has a large distance from the other the rest of the dataset. The second type is the contextual anomaly, which is given in a specific context mainly used in timeseries datasets. For instance, a temperature above 30°C during the winter season in a Nordic country. The third type of anomaly, the collective anomaly, is an ensemble of dataset points that collectively shows a different pattern. In other words, an ensemble of different patterns occurring together is the anomaly. Each member of this ensemble occurred by itself; it is not necessarily an anomaly. This type of anomaly is also very used in timeseries datasets.

The are several ways for anomaly detection. A simple statistical based approach is to identify the points that diverge from the distribution of the dataset. In machine learning, the k-nearest neighbor is a simple procedure employed for anomaly detection. This algorithm is based on the density of the data. The nearest points are determined by a distance such as the Euclidean distance or Mahalanobis distance. Another procedure employed is the k-means algorithm that relies on clusters. Data that does not belong to the clusters containing similar groups are considered anomalies.

What is semi-supervised learning?

This third paradigm of learning is a hybrid approach which uses both supervised and unsupervised learning technics. Semi-supervised learning makes use of unlabeled datasets aside from labeled datasets. Often, labeled datasets are not available, or only a few are available, which makes the unsupervised learning very useful.

Semi-supervised learning is based on the concept of training models with labeled dataset first. Then apply models on the unlabeled dataset in order to build other models that learn from the produced datasets. The pseudo-learning is a simple approach to perform the semi-supervised learning. It starts by training a model on a training dataset, which is the labeled dataset. Next, it uses this model to predict the outputs of the unlabeled dataset. Then, it merges the labeled training dataset with the unlabeled dataset. It also merges the labels of the training dataset with the model output. New formed data is employed to fit the model. This way, the model performance is enhanced, and the learning process of the data structure is improved.

What is reinforcement learning?

Reinforcement learning is based on the trial and error process, where the model learns interactively. Like supervised learning, reinforcement learning uses a mapping function between the input and output. It uses feedback from the output to correct the mapping using a reward concept. Unlike unsupervised learning where the objective is to find similarities in the datasets, reinforcement learning has a goal of defining a function that would maximize a reward. This type of learning is used in developing game strategies, for example, to define the best actions to win the game. Reinforcement learning is very handy in solving a complex problem that contains several actions that are correlated to achieve a goal. Before we present some used algorithms in reinforcement learning, let's first define the terminology used to define a reinforcement learning problem.

The reinforcement learning relies on the principles of environments, agents, states, actions and rewards, the policy as well as value. We are going to explain each of these reinforcement learning components.

Let's start first by defining the agent, which is the core component of reinforcement learning. An Agent is a component that makes actions. Basically, it is an algorithm that performs actions or models a certain concept. It can be an algorithm that simulates a game.

An action is an ensemble of several possible moves or activities that the agent can make or perform. The action is pre-defined, and the agent chooses among all these possibilities. Using the game example, action can be a list of directions such as moving right, left, up or down. It can also include the speed, fast or slow.

The state is the current situation in which the agent is. It can be a specific location or moment that places the agent in a specific relation with other elements within its environment.

The reward is the feedback that determines whether the action taken by the agent is a successful action or a failure action. In short, the reward is a measure that evaluates the success or failure of the agent's operations.

Environment is the world where the agents make the actions and operations. The agent state and action are fed to the environment that processes them. Then, it evaluates the reward. It returns the evaluated reward as well as the next state of the agent.

The policy is a scheme which the agent follows to define the next action according to the current state. The policy relates states to action in order to map the high rewarding actions.

Finally, the value represents the reward that an agent would have obtained if it performed an action in a specific state.

Now the question is how reinforcement learning use these concepts? Basically, the agent performs an action in a current state. This action is evaluated by the environment that returns a reward and a state of the agent. According to this information, another action is taken by the agent. The process is repeated in order to maximize the reward. The goal in reinforcement learning is to define the best sequence of actions that the agent should take in order to achieve its goal and maximize the reward or what is conventionally known in optimization the objective function.

Two types of reinforcement learning exist, namely the positive and negative reinforcement. The positive reinforcement consists of increasing the frequency of action when a state or a reward happens when this action is taken. In contrast, the negative reinforcement consists of increasing the frequency of an action when a reward is not received or avoided.

Most commonly used algorithms are State-Action-Reward-State-Action and Q-learning algorithm. These algorithms are usually combined with a neural network to enhance their performance. They use neural networks as agents.

How to create a model with machine learning?

As discussed earlier in this section, different types of machine learning exist. In order to choose a specific approach, supervised, unsupervised, or reinforcement learning, the problem being solved and the type of data available guide to adopting a certain approach. Supervised learning comes handy when you already have data with known output, and you try to forecast the outcome of new data. For instance, you already have a product in the market, you know the patterns and profiles of your clients, and you try to predict if new clients would be interested in that product. In contrast, unsupervised learning paradigm is useful when you ignore the desired output from your data, for example, when marketing a new product. If a combination of labeled and unlabeled data is available, then it is best to combine both supervised and unsupervised paradigms through the semi-supervised approach. Reinforcement learning is best applicable in developing computer games, robotics, automatic learning of treatment policies for healthcare, or stock market online trading. It is best applied for interactive learning processes.

The first step to start resolving a problem with machine learning is getting the data. At this step, knowledge of the problem should point toward where to get the data and what expectations regarding the form of the training dataset. The second step is identifying the features that should be used for learning. Redundancy in features might be helpful, and most current algorithms do not require independent features. Selection methods are useful tools to decrease the features being used or simply using an algorithm that is designed to deal with multiple features is preferable. This step requires an exploration of the date, estimating any missing data, and detecting the presence of outliers or noisy data. The third step is choosing an algorithm according to the convenient learning paradigm identified and the goal of the machine learning model. Often a particular algorithm would naturally be the best fit for the problem. However, it is a good practice to try many algorithms and select the best. The algorithm should be trained on the part of the data and tested against the other part for performance verification. There are different approaches to apply performance testing. One approach is to split the data into two equivalent datasets if it is a large dataset. The model can be trained on 50% of the dataset and tested on the other 50%. Another approach is to use

10-fold cross-validation, which consists of randomly splitting the data into 10 data blocks. In turn, the model is trained on 9 data block and tested on 1 one data block. This process is repeated many times, and performance testing should be used for each algorithm tested. This might be very computational expensive in particular for large dataset. This is one of the disadvantages of machine learning. One should consider finding a balance between simplicity and fitting the data. Another disadvantage is overfitting meaning that the model has higher performance on the training dataset and very low performance when tested on an independent dataset.

In this chapter, we covered the major machine learning paradigms, namely semi-supervised, unsupervised, supervised, and finally, reinforcement. We presented some methods that are used for each of these types of learning. The disadvantage of the method presented, for example, linear or logistic regression for supervised learning is based on a linear correlation between the data features and the target output. However, the majority of real worlds applications this relationship is not linear. Therefore, we need other tools to model the relationship between the inputs and outputs. A widely used tool is artificial neural networks. Moreover, these networks are often combined with traditional methods to improve their performance, as was mentioned in reinforcement learning. This tool is presented in details in the following chapter.

Chapter 2: Artificial Neural Networks

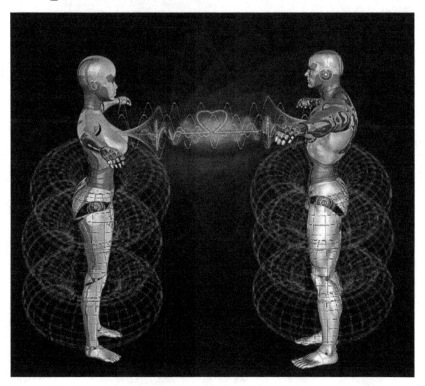

This chapter discusses the integral aspect of artificial neural networks. It also covers their component in particular activation functions and how to train an artificial neural network, as well as the different advantages of using an artificial neural network.

Definition of artificial neural network

A widely used approach in machine learning, the employment of artificial neural network is inspired by the brain system of humans. The objective of neural networks is replicating how the human brain learns. The neural network system is an ensemble of input and output layers and a hidden layer that transforms the input layer into useful information to the output layer. Usually, several hidden layers are implemented in an artificial neural network. The figure below presents an example of a neural network system composed of 2 hidden layers:

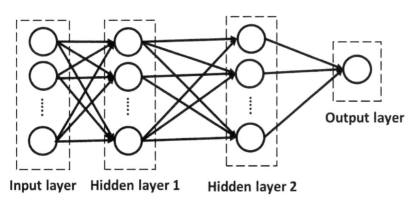

Input layer   Hidden layer 1   Hidden layer 2

Output layer

Example of an artificial neural network

Before going further and explaining how neural networks work, let's first define what is a neuron. A neuron is simply a mathematical equation expressed as the sum of the weighted inputs. Let's consider $X=\{x_1, x_2,....x_M\}$ a vector of N inputs, the neuron is a linear combination of all inputs defined as follows:

$$F(X=\{x_1, x_2,....x_M\})=w_1x_1+w_2x_2+....+w_Mx_M;$$

With $w_1, w_2,...w_M$ is the weights assigned to each input. The function F can also be represented as:

$$F(X)=WX,$$

183

With W a weight matrix and X a vector of data. The second formulation is very convenient when programming a neural network model. The weights are determined during the training procedure. In fact, training an artificial neural network means finding the optimal weights W that provide the most accurate output.

To each neuron, an activation function is applied the resulted weighted sum of inputs X. The role of the activation function is deciding whether the neuron should be activated or not according to the model's prediction. This process is applied to each layer of the network. In the next sub-sections, we will discuss in details the role and types of activation functions as well as the different types of neural networks.

What is an activation function and its role in neural network models?

Activation functions are formulated as mathematical functions. These functions are a crucial component of an artificial neural network model. For each neuron, an activation function is associated. The activation function decides whether to activate the neuron or not. For instance, let's consider the output from a neuron, which is:

$Y = \sum(weight*input) + bias.$

The output Y can be of any value. The neuron does not have any information on the reasonable range of values that Y can take. For this purpose, the activation function is implemented in the neural network to check Y values and make a decision on whether the neural connections should consider this neuron activated or not.

There are different types of activation functions. The most instinctive function is the ***step function***. This function sets a threshold and decides to activate or not activate a neuron if it exceeds a certain threshold. In other words, the output of this function is 1 if Y is greater than a threshold and 0 otherwise. Formally, the activation function is:

F='activated' or F=1; if Y> threshold

F='not-activated' or F=0; otherwise.

This activation function can be used for a classification problem where the output should be yes or no (i.e., 0 or 1). However, it has some drawbacks. For example, let's consider a set of several categories (i.e., class1, class2, ..., etc.) to which input may belong to. If this activation function is used and more than one neuron is activated, the output will be 1 for all neurons. In this case, it is hard to distinguish between the classes and decide into which class the input belong to because all neuron outputs are 1. In short, the step function does not support multiple output values and classification into several classes.

Linear activation function, unlike the step function, provides a range of activation values. It computes an output that is proportional to the input. Formally:

F(X)=WX, where X is the input.

This function supports several outputs rather than just a 1 or 0 values. This function, because it is linear, does not support backpropagation for model training. Backpropagation is the process that relies on function derivative or gradient to update the parameters, in particular, the weights. The derivative (i.e., gradient) of the linear activation function is a constant which is equal to W and is not related to changes in the input X. Therefore, it does not provide information on which weights applied to the input can give accurate predictions.

Moreover, all layers can be reduced to one layer when using the linear function. The fact that all layers are using a linear function, the final layer is a linear function of the first layer. So, no matter how many layers are used in the neural network, they are equivalent to the first layer, and there is no point of using multiple layers. A neural network with multiple layers connected with a linear activation function is just a linear regression model that cannot support the complexity of input data.

The majority of neural networks use non-linear activation functions because, in the majority of real-world applications, relations between the output and the input features are non-linear. The non-linear functions allow the neural network to map complex patterns between the inputs and the outputs. They also allow the neural network to learn the complex process that governs complex data or high dimension data such as images, audios, among others. The non-linear functions allow overcoming the drawbacks of linear functions and step functions. They support backpropagation (i.e., the derivative is not a constant and depends on the changes of the input) and stacking several layers (i.e., the combination of non-linear functions is non-linear). Several non-linear functions exist and can be used within a neural network. In this book, we are going to cover the most commonly used non-linear activation functions in machine learning applications.

The **sigmoid function** is one of the most used activation functions within an artificial neural network. Formally, a sigmoid function is equal to the inverse of the sum of 1 and the exponential of inputs:

$$F(X)=1/(1+exp(-X))$$

Outputs of a sigmoid function are bounded by 0 and 1. More precisely, the outputs take any value between 0 and 1 and provide clear predictions. In fact, when the X is greater than 2 or lower than -2, the value of Y is close to the edge of the curve (i.e., closer to 0 or 1).

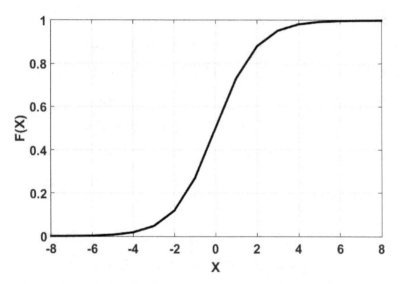

Sigmoid activation function

The disadvantage of this activation function, as we can see from the figure above, is the small change in the output for input values under -4 and above 4. This problem is called '*vanishing gradient*' which means that the gradient is very small on horizontal extremes of the curve. This makes a neural network using the sigmoid function, learning very slow when they approach the edges and computational expensive.

The **tanh function** is another activation function used that is similar to the sigmoid function. The mathematical formulation of this function is:

$$F(X)=\tanh(X)=[2/(1+\exp(-2X)]-1.$$

This function is a scaled sigmoid function. Therefore, it has the same characteristics as the sigmoid function. However, the outputs of this function range between -1 and 1, and the gradient are more pronounced than the gradient of the sigmoid function. Unlike the sigmoid function, the tanh function is zero-centered, which makes it very useful for inputs with negative, neutral, and positive values. The drawback of this function, as for the sigmoid function, is the vanishing gradient issue and computationally expensive.

The **Rectified Linear Unit function** or what is known as **ReLu function,** is also a widely used activation function, which is computationally efficient. This function is efficient and allows the neural network to converge quickly compared to the sigmoid and tanh function because it uses simple mathematical formulations. ReLu returns X as output if X is positive or 0 otherwise. Formally, this activation function is formulated as

F(X)=max(0,X).

This activation function is not bounded and takes values from 0 to +inf. Although it has a similar shape as a linear function (i.e., this function is equal to identity for positive values), the ReLu function has a derivative. The drawback of the ReLu is that the derivative (i.e., the gradient) is 0 when the inputs are negative. This means as for the linear functions, the backpropagation cannot be processed, and the neural network cannot learn unless the inputs are greater than 0. This aspect of the ReLu, gradient equal to 0 when the inputs are negative, is called dying ReLu problem.

To prevent the dying ReLu problem, two ReLu variations can be used, namely the **Leaky ReLu function** and the **Parametric ReLu function**. The Leakey ReLu function returns as output the maximum of X and X by 0.1. In other words, the leaky ReLu is equal to the identity function when X is greater than 0 and is equal to the product of 0.1 and X when X is less than zero. This function is provided as follows:

F(X)=max (0.1*X, X)

This function has a small positive gradient which 0.1 when X has negative values, which make this function support backpropagation for negative values. However, it may not provide a consistent prediction for these negative values.

The parametric ReLu function is similar to the Leaky ReLu function, that takes the gradient as a parameter to the neural network to define the output when X is negative. The mathematical formulation of this function is as follows:

$$F(X)=\max (aX, X)$$

There are other variations of the ReLu function such as the *exponential linear ReLu*. This function, unlike the other variations of the ReLu the Leaky ReLu and parametric ReLu, has a log curve for negative values of X instead of the linear curves like the Leaky ReLu and the parametric ReLu functions. The downside of this function is it saturates for large negative values of X. Other variations exist which all relies on the same concept of defining a gradient greater than 0 when X has negative values.

The *Softmax function* is another type of activation function used differently than the one presented previously. This function is usually applied only to the output layer when a classification of the inputs into several different classes is needed. In fact, the Softmax function supports several classes and provides the probability of input to belong to a specific class. It normalizes outputs of every category between 0 and 1 then divides by their sum to provide that probability.

Given all these activation functions, where each one has its pros and cons, the question now which one should be used in a neural network? The answer is simply having a better understanding of the problem in hand will help guide into a specific activation function, especially if the characteristics of the function being approximated are known beforehand. For instance, a sigmoid function is a good choice for a classification problem. In case the nature of the function being approximated is unknown, it is highly recommended to start with a ReLu function than try other activation function. Overall, ReLu function works well for a wide range of applications. It is an ongoing research, and you may try your own activation function.

An important aspect of choosing an activation function is sparsity of the activation. Sparsity means that not all neurons are activated. This is a desired characteristic in a neural network because it makes the network learns faster and less prone to overfitting. Let's imagine a large neural network with multiple neurons if all neurons were activated; it means all these neurons are processed to describe the final output. This makes the neural network very dense and computationally exhaustive to process. The sigmoid and the tanh activation functions have this property of activating almost all neurons, which makes them computationally inefficient unlike the ReLu function and its variations that cause the inactivation of some negative values. That is the reason why it is recommended to start with the ReLu function when approximating a function with unknown characteristics.

What are the types of artificial neural networks?

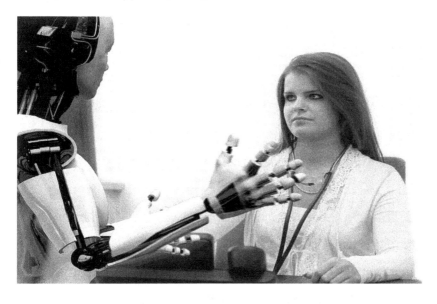

Several categories of artificial neural networks with different properties and complexities exist. The first and simplest neural network developed is the perceptron. The **perceptron** computes the sum of the inputs, applies an activation function, and provide the result to the output layer.

Another old and simple approach is the ***feedforward neural network***. This type of artificial neural network has only one single layer. It is a category that is fully connected to the following layer where each node is attached to the others. It propagates the information in one direction from the inputs to the outputs through the hidden layer. This process is known as the front propagated wave that usually uses what is called the activation function. This activation function processes the data in each node of the layers. This neural network returns a sum of weights by the inputs calculated according to the hidden layer's activation function. The category of feedforward neural network usually uses the backpropagation method for the training process and the logistic function as an activation function.

Several other neural networks are a derivation of this type of networks. For example, ***the radial basis function neural*** network. This is a feedforward neural network that depends on the radial basis function instead of the logistic function. This type of neural networks has two layers, wherein the inner layer, the features, and radial basis function are combined. The radial function computes the distance of each point to the relative center. This neural network is useful for continuous values to evaluate the distance from the target value.

In contrast, the logistic function is used for mapping arbitrary binary values (i.e., 0 or 1; yes or no). ***Deep feedforward neural networks*** are a multilayer feedforward neural network. They became the most commonly used neural network types used in machine learning as they yield better results. A new type of learning called deep learning has emerged from this type of neural networks.

Recurrent neural networks are another category that uses a different type of nodes. Like a feedforward neural network, each hidden layer processes the information to the next layer. However, outputs of the hidden layers are saved and processed back to the previous layer. Basically, the first layer, comprised of the input layer, is processed as the product of the sum of the weighted features. The recurrent process is applied in hidden layers. At each step, every node will save information from the previous step. It actually uses memory, while the computation is running. In short, the recurrent neural network uses forward propagation and backpropagation to self-learn from the previous timesteps to improve the predictions. In other words, information is processed in two directions, unlike the feedforward neural networks.

A **multilayer perceptron or multilayer neural network** is a neural network that has at least three or more layers. This category of networks is fully connected where every node is attached to all other nodes in the following layers.

Convolutional neural networks are typically useful for image classification or recognition. The processing used by this type of artificial neural network is designed to deal with pixel data. The convolutional neural networks are a multi-layer network that is based on convolutions, which apply filters for neuron activation. When the same filter is applied to a neuron, it leads to an activation of the same feature and results in what is called a feature map. The feature map reflects the strength and importance of a feature of input data.

Modular neural networks are formed from more than one connected neural network. These networks rely on the concept of 'divide and conquer.' They are handy for very complex problems because they allow combining different types of neural networks. Therefore, they allow combining the strengths of a different neural network to solve a complex problem where each neural network can handle a specific task.

How to train an artificial neural network?

As explained at the beginning of this chapter, neural networks compute a weighted sum of inputs and apply an activation function at each layer. Then it provides the final result to the output layer. This procedure is commonly named as forward propagation. In order to train these artificial neural networks, weights need to be optimized to obtain the optimal weights that produce the most accurate outputs. The process of the training an artificial neural network is as follows:

1. Initialize the weights
2. Apply the forward propagation process
3. Evaluate the neural network performance
4. Apply the backward propagation process
5. Update the weights
6. Repeat the steps from step 2 until it attains a maximum number of iterations, or neural network performance does not improve.

As we can see from the steps of training an artificial neural network presented above, we need a performance measure that describes how accurate the neural network is. This function is called the loss function or cost function. This function can be the same as the cost function we presented in the previous chapter:

$$J = (1/N) * \sum (y_{predicted} - y_{target})^2$$

Where N: the number of outputs, $y_{predicted}$: the output and y_{target} : the true value of the output. This function provides the error of the neural network. Small values of J reflect the high accuracy of the neural network.

So far, we defined loss function and how the neural network works in general. Now, let's go into the details for each step of the training process.

Let's consider a set of inputs X and outputs Y. We initialize W (i.e., weights) and B (i.e., bias) as a null matrix. The next step is to apply the feed forward propagation that consists of feeding each layer of the artificial neural network with the sum of the weights by the inputs and the bias. Let's consider that we have two layers. We can calculate the first hidden layer's output using the following equation:

$$Z_1 = W_1 * X + b_1$$

where W_1 and b_1 are the parameters of the neural network as the weights and bias of the first layer, respectively.

Next, we apply the activation function F_1, that can be any activation from the function presented previously in this chapter:

$$A_1 = F_1(Z_1).$$

The result is the output of the first layer, which is then is feed to the next layer as:

$$Z_2 = W_2 * A_1 + b_2$$

with W_2 and b_2 are the weights and bias of the second layer, respectively.

To this result, we apply an activation function F_2:

$$A_2 = F_2(Z_2).$$

Now A2 is supposed to be the output of the artificial neural network. The activation function F1 and F2 might be the same activation function or different activation function depending on the dataset and the expected output.

After the feedforward propagation, we compare the neural network output against the target output with the loss function. It is highly likely the difference between the estimated output and the actual values at this stage is very high. Therefore, we have to adjust the weights through the backpropagation process. We calculate the gradient of each activation function concerning biases and weights. We start by evaluating the derivative of the last layer, then the layer before this layer on so on until the input layer. Then update the weights according to the gradient or the derivative of the activation function. Applying these steps to our example of two layers neural network it provides:

$$W2 = W2 - \alpha^*(dF2(W, b)/dW)$$
$$B2 = b2 - \alpha^*(dF2(W, b)/db)$$
$$W1 = W1 - \alpha^*(dF2(W, b)/dW)$$
$$B1 = b1 - \alpha^*(dF2(W, b)/db)$$

The parameter α is the learning rate parameter. This parameter determines the rate by which the weights are updated. The process that we just describe here is called the gradient descent algorithm. The process is repeated until it attains a pre-fixed maximum number of iterations. In chapter 4, we will develop an example to illustrate a perceptron and multi-layer neural network by following similar steps using Python. We will develop a classifier based on an artificial neural network. Now, let's explore the pros of using an artificial neural network for machine learning application.

Artificial neural network: pros and cons of use

Nowadays, artificial neural networks are applied in almost every domain. Research in the domain of artificial neural networks is very active, and several neural networks immerged to take advantage of the full potential of this Artificial intelligence approach. Artificial neural networks have several advantages.

Artificial neural networks are able to map structures and learn from the data faster. They are also able to map the complex structure and connections that relate the outputs to the input datasets, which is the case in many real-life applications. Once an artificial neural network is developed and trained, it can be generalized. In other words, it can be applied to map relationships between data that it has not been exposed to or to make predictions for new datasets. Moreover, the artificial neural network does not make any assumptions of the structure or the distribution of the input data. It does not impose specific conditions on the data or assumptions on the relationship in the data, unlike traditional statistical methods. The fact that artificial neural networks can handle a large amount of data makes them an appealing tool. Artificial neural networks are a non-parametric approach which allows developing a model with a reduced error that is caused by the estimation of the parameters. Although these appealing characteristics of artificial neural networks, they suffer from some drawbacks.

The downside of artificial neural networks is that they often operate as a black box. This means that we cannot fully understand the relationship between the inputs and outputs and the interdependence between specific input variables and the output. In other words, we cannot detect how much each input variable impacts the output. The training process can be computationally inefficient. We can overcome this problem by using parallel computing and taking advantage of the computation power of computers by using proper coding.

Chapter 3: Python for Machine Learning

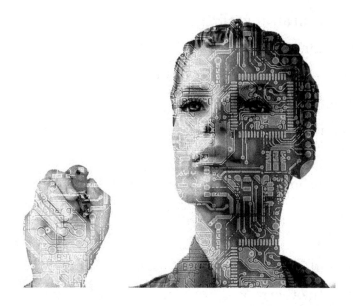

In order to use machine learning, we need a programming language to provide instruction to the machine to execute the code. In this section, we are going to learn the basics of the Python language, how to install and launch python. We are also going to learn some Python syntax and some useful tools to run Python. We also cover some basic Python libraries that useful for machine learning. These libraries will be used in the next chapter to develop machine learning applications. First of all, why we would use Python and not another programming language?

Why use Python for machine learning?

Python is a programming language extensively used for many reasons. One main reason it is a free and open source language, which means it is accessible for everybody. Although it is free, it is community-based language, meaning that is developed and supported by a community that gathers its effort through the internet to improve the language features. Other reasons people would use Python are 1) quality as a readable language with a simple syntax, 2) program portability to any operating system (e.g. Windows , Unix) without or with little modifications,3)Speed of execution: Python does not need compilation and run faster than similar programming languages, 4) Component integration which means that Python can be integrated with other programs, can be called from C and C++ libraries, or call another programming language. Python comes with basic and powerful standard operations as well as advanced pre-coded libraries like Numpy for numeric programming. Another advantage of Python is automatic memory management and does not require variable and size declaration. Moreover, Python allows developing different application such as developing Graphical User Interface (GUI), doing numeric programming, do game programming, database programming, internet scripting, and much more. In this book section, we will focus on how to do numeric programming for machine learning applications and how to get started with Python.

How to Get started with Python?

Python, a scripting language, and like any other programming languages, it needs an interpreter. The latter is a program which executes other language programs. As its name indicates, it works as an interpreter for computer hardware to execute the instructions of a Python programming. Python comes as a software package and can be downloaded from Python's website: *www.python.org*. When installing Python, the interpreter is usually an executable program. Note that if you use UNIX and LUNIX, Python might be already installed and probably is in the /usr directory. Now that you have Python installed let's explore how we can run some basic code.

To run Python, you can open your operating system's prompt (on Windows open a DOS console Window) and type python. If it does not work, it means that you don't have python in Shell's path Environment variable. In this case, you should type the full path of the Python executable. On Windows, it should be something similar to C:\Python3.7\python and in UNIX or LUNIX is installed in the bin folder: /usr/local/bin/python (or /usr/bin/python).

When you launch Python, it provides two lines of information with the first line is the Python version used as in the example below:

> Python 3.7.1 (default, Dec 10 2018, 22:54:23) [MSC v.1915 64 bit (AMD64)] :: Anaconda, Inc. on win32
>
> Type "help", "copyright", "credits" or "license" for more

information.

> \>\>\>

Once a session is launched, Python prompts >>> which means it is ready. It is ready to run line codes you write in. The following is an example of printing statement:

> \>\>\> print('Hello World !')
>
> Hello World !
>
> \>\>\>

When running Python in an interactive session as we did, it displays the results after >>> as shown in the example. The code is executed interactively. To exit the interactive Python session type Ctrl-Z on Windows or Ctrl-D on Unix/Lunix machine.

Now we learned how to launch Python and run codes in an interactive session. This is a good way to experiment and test codes. However, the code is never saved and need to be typed again to run the statement again. To store the code, we need to type it in a file called module. Files that contain Python statements are called modules. These files have an extension '.py.' The module can be executed simply by typing the module name. A text editor like Notepad++ can be used to create the module files. For instance, let's create a module named *text.py* that prints 'Hello World,' and calculates 3^2. The file should contain the following statements:

```
print ('Hello World! ')
print ('3^2 equal to ' 3**2)
```

To run this module, in the operating system's prompt, type the following command line:

```
python test.py
```

If this command line does not work, you should type the full path of Python's executable and the full path of the test.py file. You can also change the working directory by typing cd full path of the test.py file, then type python test.py. Changing the working directory to the directory where you saved the modules is a good way to avoid typing the full path of the modules every time you are running the module. The output is:

```
C:\Users>python C:\Users\test.py
Hello World!
3^2 equal to 9
```

When we run the module test.py, the results are displayed in the operating system's prompt and go away as the prompt is closed. To store the results in a file, we can use a shell syntax by typing:

python test.py > save.txt

The output of test.py is redirected and saved in the save.txt file. In the next sections, we are going to learn Python syntax. For now, we are going to use the command line to explore Python syntax. Later in the current chapter, we will learn how to set and use some powerful platforms for Python programming.

Python syntax

Before we learn some Python syntax, we are going to explore the main types of data that can be used in Python and how a program is structured. A program is a set of modules which are a series of statements that contains expressions. These expressions create and process objects which are variables that represent data.

Python Variables

In Python, we can use built-in objects, namely numbers, strings, lists, dictionaries, tuples, and files. Python supports the usual numeric types the integer and float as well as complex numbers. Strings are character chain whereas lists and dictionaries are an ensemble of other objects that can be a number or a string or other lists or dictionaries. Lists and dictionaries are indexed and can be iterated through. The main difference between lists and dictionaries is the way items are stored and how they can be fetched. Items in a list are ordered and can be fetched by position whereas they are stored and fetched in dictionaries by key. Tuples like lists are positionally ordered set of objects. Finally, Python allows also creating and reading files as objects. Python provides all the tools and mathematical functions to process these objects. In this book, we will focus on the number variables and how to process them as we won't need the other variables for basic machine learning applications.

Python does not require variable declaration, or size or type declaration. Variables are created once they are assigned a value. For example:

>>> x=5
>>> print (x)
5
>>> x= 'Hello World ! '
Hello World !

In the example above, x was assigned a number then it was assigned a string. In fact, Python allows changing the type of variables after they are declared. We can verify the type of any Python object using the type() function.

>>> x, y, z=10,'Banana,2.4
>>> print (type(x))
<class 'int '>
>>> print(type(y))
<class 'str '>
>>> print (type(z))
<class 'float '>

To declare a string variable, both single and double quotes can be used.

To name a Python variable, only alpha-numeric characters and underscores can be used (e.g., A_9). Note that the variable names are case-sensitive and should not start with a number. For instance, price, Price, and PRICE are three different variables. Multiple variables can be declared in one line, as seen in the example above.

Number Variables

Python allows three numeric types: int (for integer), float and complex. Integers are positive or negative numbers without decimals of unlimited length. Floats are negative or positive numbers with decimals. Complex numbers are expressed with a 'j' for the imaginary part as follows:

```
>>> x=2+5j
>>> print(type(x))
<class 'complex '>
```

We can convert from one number type to another type with int(), float() and complex() functions. Note that you cannot convert a complex number to another type.

Python has built-in mathematic operators that allow doing the basic operations such as addition, multiplication, and subtraction. It also has the power function. No, if we want to process a set of values, we would want to store them in one single object as a list. To define a list, we type the set of values separated by a comma between square brackets:

>>> A=[10,20,30,40,50]

We can select one element by typing the element index between the square brackets:

>>> print (A[1])

20

We can also slicer notation to select several elements. For example, displaying the 2nd to 4th element:

>>> print(A[1:4])

[20,30,40]

Note that indexing in Python start with 0 that is the index of the first element is 0. When using the slicer notation, the element of the second index is not included as in the example above. The value of A[4] is 50 and is not included in the output. To verify the dimension of an array, the len() function can be used.
The disadvantage of using lists to store a set of variables is Python does not allow to apply the mathematical operations on lists. Let's say we want to add a constant variable to the list X we created. We have to iterate over all the list elements and add the constant variable. However, there is a Numpy library that allows to create an array of the same type and do the basic

mathematical operations. The Numpy arrays are different from the basic list arrays of Python as the Numpy arrays allow only to store variables of the same type. The Nympy library is useful in machine learning to create input, output variables, and perform necessary calculations.

In order to be able to exploit the built-in function of the Numpy library, we must import the library into the workspace by typing:

>>> import numpy as np

Use the command **pip -install "numpy"** to install this toolbox, if it is not already installed in the system.

To create an array, we type:

>>> A=np.array([10,20,30,40])

Now, we can add, multiply or subtract a constant value from the array X by using the simple mathematical operators:

```
>>> X=np.array([1,2,3,4]) # Creating a vector
>>> print(X)
[1 2 3 4]
>>> X=X+5 # Adding 5 to all elements
>>> print(X)
[6 7 8 9]
>>> X=X*10 # Multiplying all elements by 10
>>> print (X)
```

[60 70 80 90]

>>> X=X-10 # Subtracting 10 from all elements

>>> print (X)

[50 60 70 80]

>>> X=X**2 # Square of all elements

>>> print (X)

[2500 3600 4900 6400]

Use the functions max() and min() to arrive at the array's minimum and maximum values. The function sum() provide the sum of elements of the same array. We can also apply these operators (+,*, -,/) on two arrays. These operators are applied element by element when executed on arrays such as in the example below:

>>> Y=np.array([1,2,3,4]) # Create a second array

>>> print (Y)

[1 2 3 4]

>>> X+Y

array([2501, 3602, 4903, 6404])

>>> X*Y

array(2500, 7200, 14700, 25600])

>>> X/Y

array([2500. , 1800. , 1633.333333, 1600.])

>>> X-Y

array([2499, 3598, 4897, 6396])

Usually, in machine learning, we have multiple features of inputs. For example, if a machine learning program predicting human age according to the height and weight to be developed and a 100 of height and weight records form the dataset. It is usually more convenient to store these values as a matrix where each row is a record of height and weight. That is if the dimension of the matrix is 100 by 2. To do so in Python, we can create a multi-dimension array as follows:

>>>A=np.array([[10,20],[30,40]])

In this example A is 2x2 matrix where the first line is [10,20] and the second line is [30,40]. To select an element, we use the same indexing as for the array as follows:

>>> X[0] # first row of the matrix
array([10,20])
>>> X[0][1] # first row second column of the matrix
20

To verify the matrix's dimension, you can just use the shape() function as follows:

>>> X.shape
(2,2)
>>> X.shape[0] # number or rows
2

```
>>> X.shape[1] # number of columns
2
```

We will cover in details the Numpy library later in this chapter.

In the next section, we are going to learn how to iterate through an array or matrix and how to use the if else statements.

If test and loops in Python

Before learning how to code loops and If statements, it is important to mention that indentations are very crucial when programming with Python. Indentations in Python is used to indicate a block of code. If you skip indentation, it will give an error:

```
>>> if 10>5:
... print('YES')
File "<stdin>", line 2
  print('YES')
    ^
IndentationError: expected an indented block
```

Therefore, whenever using a loop or If the statement, you must use indentation for the instructions used within these statements.

If statements allow running a set of instructions if a condition is met. It can contain other if statements.

The general format is as follows:

```
if <condition1>:      # if test
        <statements1># block of instructions to run when
condition1 is true
    elif <condition2>: # optional or additional condition
        <statements2>#Instructions to run when
condition2 is true
    else:
        <statements3> Instructions to run otherwise
```

For example, let's verify if all values stored in X are superior to 10 and display true otherwise display false.

```
>>> if all(X>10):
...      print('true')
... else:
...      print('false')
...
    true
```

Python allows two loop commands, namely the while loop and for a loop. The for loop is used when the number of iterations is known beforehand. On the contrary, the while loop is used when the number of iterations is unknown and executes a statement as long as a condition is satisfied. They both yield the same results but as a rule of thumb always use for a loop when you know exactly the number of iterations. The reason behind this rule is to avoid infinite loops.

The general format of a for loop is:

```
for <element> in <object>: # assign object items to element
    <statements> # block of statements
```

Python allows stopping running a for loop if a condition is satisfied and an optional else block that runs once the loop is over. A continue statement is also optional that forces the loop to go from the top and skip the code if a condition is satisfied. The format is as follows:

```
for <element> in <object>: # assign object items to element
    <statements1> # block of statements
    if <condition1>: break # Exit loop and skip else
    if <condition2>: continue # Go to the top and skip the next block
else:
    <statements2> # if condition1 is not satisfied and did not hit break
```

Below is a for loop example, displaying each element in the array X that we created before:

```
>>> for i in X:
...     print (i)
2500
3600
4900
6400
```

Because the loop we coded is simple we can type it in one single line as follows:

```
>>> for i in X: print(i)
...
2500
3600
4900
6400
```

The while loop syntax is similar to the for loop with the exception that the header is a test or condition that force the loop to run until that condition is no longer satisfied. The general format of While loop is:

```
while <constraint>: # condition to run the loop
        <statements> # body of the loop
else:
        <statements> # block to run when exit the loop
```

Like the for loop, we can add if tests to exit or continue the loop with break and continue statements as follows:

```
while <condition1>: # assign object items to element
        <statements1> # block of statements
        if <condition2>: break # Exit loop and skip else
        if <condition3>: continue # Continues the loop
from the loop top
    else:
            <statements2># if condition2 is not satisfied and
    did not hit break
```

For example, we let's display values until the variable j is no longer less than 5 and we are going to exit the loop if i is equal to 4:

```
>>>j=1
>>> while j<5:
...      print(j)
...      if j==4:
...              break
...      j+=1
1
2
3
4
```

The statements i+=1 increments the values of i by 1 at each iteration. It is very important to increase the value of i; otherwise, the loop will never exit.

Now that we have learned how to manipulate arrays and use loops, in the next section, we will learn how to develop functions that allow running the same code multiple times for different inputs.

Functions in Python

Before diving into function coding, it is worthwhile to know how to document the codes in order to help understand the program and make it more readable. Usually, this is done by making comments in the script. Python recognizes comments lines according to the symbol '#' at the beginning of a line or statement to indicate to the interpreter that it is a comment. When executing the program, Python will ignore everything that follows # symbol. For example:

```
>>> print ('Hello World! ') # This a test comment
Hello World !
```

To add multiple comments, # should be added at each line:

```
>>># This is comment number 1
>>> # This is comment number 2
```

We can also add multiple comments in different lines by using """" at the first line and at the last line:

```
>>> """
... This a comment
... Example expanding
... on three lines
... """
```

Functions are very useful when you have repetitive tasks to run in a program. Instead of typing the same code several times with different object values, we can call a function with different object values as inputs several times. Python already has some useful built-in function like the one we used so far in the examples: print(), max(), etc.. Now we are going to learn how we can define and create different functions. The general format of a function is:

```
def function_name (inputs):
        <statements>
```

To call a function, we can use simply the following statement function_name (inputs).
For example, let's develop a simple function which displays 'Hello world!'.

```
>>> def first_function():
...        print('Hello World!)
```

```
...
>>>first_function()
Hello World!
```

Function, as shown in the general format, can take inputs and return outputs with the return statement. For instance, we can create a function that computes, prints, and returns the sum of two variables.

```
>>> def sum_function(a,b):
...      c=a+b
...      print(' The sum of', a 'and', b ' is: ' , c)
...      return c
...
sum_function(3,5)
The sum of 3 and 5 is: 8
8
```

Note that a function can take as many as inputs as needed separated by comma and returned value can be stored in an object as follows:

```
>>> c=sum_function(3,5)
8
>>> print(c)
8
```

We can also create a function with default input values:

```
>>> def sum_function(a=2, b=1):
...         return a+b
```

By calling this function without any inputs, it will run with the default values

```
>>> c=sum_function()
>>> print (c)
3
```

Functions can be saved in a separate file with an .py extension as a module. A module general contains several functions and can be imported to the working space using the import statement.

We can save, using a text editor, the function sum_function() we defined before in a file called mymodule.py. To use the function, we import mymodule then call the function as follows:

```
>>> import mymodule
>>> mymodule.sum_function()
3
```

Modules can also contain variables of any type. In the file mymodule.py, we save, for example:

```
My_list=[ 1,2,3,4]
```

After importing the mymodule, we can access the list defined as follows:

```
>>>a=mymodule.My_list
>>>print(a)
```

We can also create alias for the module when they are imported. For example:

```
>>> import mymodule as md
>>>a=md.My_list
>>> print(a)
```

Now that we have learned the basic syntax of Python and how to develop modules, let's explore some useful platform that allows interactive Python programming easily.

Useful Platforms for Python Programming

Now, let's learn how to use some tools that allow interactive programming and also save the working environment. One powerful platform available is Anaconda. This platform is free and can be downloaded from the website anaconda.com/distribution. This platform comes with multiple open source packages and the Pip package to install other packages automatically using the pip install command. To run Python with Anaconda, you can run the Anaconda prompt and type python like how we used the Operating's system prompt or using Jupyter Notebook, which we will use throughout the rest of the book.

The web application allowing interactive programming is the Jupyter Notebook, which is open source. It supports different programming languages, including Python. It can be used for different applications like data cleaning, statistical modeling, and machine learning, among others. It is available on the website www.jupyter.org. However, as mentioned before, Jupyter Notebook is available within the Anaconda platform and can be launched from the Anaconda Navigator. On windows research bar, type Anaconda and open Anaconda Navigator and Launch Jupyter Notebook. Then, you can select Python 3 in the New tab under Notebook option. This should redirect you to a new tab in the internet Navigator as follows:

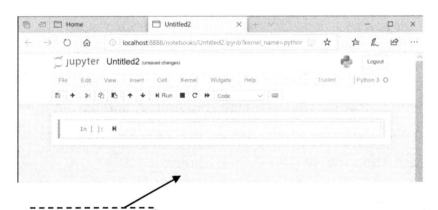

Ju Type code here llows running Python code interactively as we did with the Operating's prompt system but also to save notebook to use it later or export it as Python file or as other formats. In the file menu, there is a download as an option which provides different formats. It allows exporting the notebook in HTML, LaTeX, PDF, RevealJS, Markdown, ReStructed Text or Executable scrip formats.

To run the code in a cell, you can click 'run' tab or type Shift-Enter. By default, when you open a new notebook, there is only one cell. When you run code in this cell, it creates automatically another cell and so on. All variables created in the cells are shared in the environment. This is useful when importing libraries. In short, you don't have to import the libraries every time you want to use them once they are imported in the beginning or redefine the variables.

The Jupyter notebook is a very handy tool to share live code with other parties. Os includes several options that support that. For example, it allows deleting an output of a cell which allows for cleaning the code when sharing it with other parties. Now, that you have learned the basic syntax of Python and how to use Jupyter Notebook, in the next section, we are going to present some useful and widely used Python libraries.

What are the Python libraries that are useful for machine learning applications?

The Numpy library that we already explored in this chapter is a powerful library for scientific and numerical computing in Python. This library allows processing arrays. To install this library, you can use the following statement in Jupyter Notebook:

```
pip install numpy
```

Another widely used library is pandas, which fosters the easy management of data structures. It is also a Python package which is an open source, administering a data analysis tool that has a high performance. The pandas package uses the features available of the NumPy library.

The Pandas library allows for handling of dataframes objects. It provides tools to import data into data objects from any file formats. It provides tools to detect missing data as well as reshaping datasets. It allows deleting and inserting new elements from or to a dataset. It also allows to aggregate, transform the data merging, and joining datasets.

The Pandas package supports three structures of data, which are series, dataframe, and Panel. Series are a one-dimensional homogenous array like arrays in the Numpy library. Dataframe is multidimensional data that has a tabular structure that

227

contains a series of different types. They are indexed as rows and columns. This is the widely used structure and the one we will use in the machine learning applications in the next chapter of this book along with the series. The panel is generally a three-dimensional array.

To use the pandas library, we need to import it first:

```
import pandas as pd
```

Note here we imported pandas library and we gave the module an alias pd. To use any function from this library, we need to access it as pd.function_name. Let's create an empty series.

```
Test_series=pd.Series()
print(Test_series)
```

The output is :

```
Series([], dtype: float64)
```

The result is an empty series object with has a float type. We can create a serie object from array as follows:

```
import numpy as np
data=np.array([0,1,2,3,4])
test_series1=pd.Series(data)
print(test_series1)
```

The result this time is as follows:

```
0  0
1  1
```

```
2  2
3  3
4  4
dtype: int32
```

Note here that the first column is the index of each element of the array and second column are the data and the data type is integer (int32).

The dataframe structure is in tabular form. As we did with series, we can create a dataframe as follows:

Test_dt=pd.DataFrame()

print(Test_dt)

The returned dataframe object is as presented below:

```
Empty DataFrame
Columns: []
Index: []
```

We usually generate a new dataframe object using the previous data as follows:

data={'Age': [20,30,40,50,60,70,80],

'Name':['Bob','Brian','John','Chris','James','Steve','Peter']
}

Indiv_dt=pd.DataFrame(data)

print(Indiv_dt)

The dataframe object is as presented below:

```
     Age   Name
0    20    Bob
1    30    Brian
2    40    John
3    50    Chris
4    60    James
5    70    Steve
6    80    Peter
```

We can retrieve a column from the dataframe by using the index of the column. Let's print, for example, the age column:

> print(Indiv_dt['Age'])

This would return:

```
0    20
1    30
2    40
3    50
4    60
5    70
6    80
Name: Age, dtype: int64
```

We can delete and add columns or rows with function drop(),
pop() or del(). We can also visualize the first 5 rows by calling
the head() function:

    print(Indiv_dt.head())

This returns the first rows of the dataframe:

	Age	Name
0	20	Bob
1	30	Brian
2	40	John
3	50	Chris
4	60	James

We can visualize the last elements with the tail() function :

    print(Indiv_dt.tail())

It returns the 5 last elements of the dataframe:

	Age	Name
2	40	John
3	50	Chris
4	60	James
5	70	Steve
6	80	Peter

These functions are very handy to explore large dataset. We
can check the size with the size function:

    Indiv_dt.size

It returns 14, which is the number of elements of the dataframe object. In this example, it has 7 values of the variable age and 7 values of the variable name. For more accurate information about the shape of the dataset, we can use the shape function.

Indiv_dt.shape

This function returns (7, 2) which we have 7 rows and 2 columns.

Pandas library has the basic statistics functions listed below:

- Sum of values as *sum()*
- Cumulative sum as *cumsum()*
- Cumulative product as *cumprod()*
- Standard deviation as *std()*
- Average as *mean()*
- Median as *median()*
- Minimum value as min()
- Maximum value as max()
- Absolute value as abs()
- Mode of the dataset as mode()

The pandas library provide a function that describes the dataframe, which is the describe() function. For example, let's apply this function to the dataframe we created:

```
print(Indiv_dt.describe())
```

This function returns:

```
       Age
count  7.0
mean   50.0
std    21.6
min    20.0
25%    35.0
50%    50.0
75%    65.0
max    80.0
```

The describe function returns the basic statistics of the dataframe. Note here that we have two variables or two columns in the dataframe. The describe provided the summary statistics only for the age because it is a numerical variable. The name column was ignored.

Functions can be applied to a subset of all rows of a dataframe using the function apply(). This function allows applying a function to the rows of a dataframe.

We can reindex the columns of the dataframe as another dataframe with the reindex function. We can also rename the labels of the columns with the rename() function.

The pandas library is very useful in detecting missing values. In data analysis and machine learning, detecting missing values is a crucial step because it affects the analysis and accuracy of the final results. Let's create a dataframe with missing values and let's present how these data can be handled with pandas:

dt=pd.DataFrame(np.random.randn(5,3),index=[1,2,3,4,5],colu mns=[1,2,3])
  dt=dt.reindex([1,2,3,4,5,6,7,8])

The first statement creates a dataframe with 5 rows and 3 columns from random values. By reindexing the dataframe, we created missing values as presented in the output table below:

	1	2	3
1	-2.29	0.18	0.89
2	-0.72	-0.53	-1.72
3	0.75	0.95	0.46
4	-0.33	1.41	1.17
5	0.9	1.2	0.8
6	NaN	NaN	NaN
7	NaN	NaN	NaN
8	NaN	NaN	NaN

Pandas library has to major function isnull() and notnull() to check the presence of missing values. If we use the isnull()

function, it returns False or True for each element in the dataframe as follows: dt.isnull()

	1	2	3
1	False	False	False
2	False	False	False
3	False	False	False
4	False	False	False
5	False	False	False
6	True	True	True
7	True	True	True
8	True	True	True

This function returns True for the missing data and false otherwise. The notnull() function would return an opposite output, which means it returns False for the missing data and True otherwise. By applying notnull() function to the dataframe, we created it returns:

	1	2	3
1	True	True	True
2	True	True	True
3	True	True	True
4	True	True	True
5	True	True	True
6	False	False	False

7	False	False	False
8	False	False	False

If we apply the basic mathematical operation like the sum function, it will return NaN as a result of missing values present in the data. Therefore, we need either to remove or estimate the missing values. The pandas library offers two function to fill the missing values namely fill or pad and backfill methods. To apply these methods, we should use the fillna() function as follows:

```
print (dt.fillna(method='pad'))
```

This function returns:

	1	2	3
1	-2.289485	0.178246	0.894550
2	-0.724545	-0.531302	-1.720398
3	0.745967	0.954951	0.463451
4	-0.330040	1.407060	1.169614
5	-0.330040	1.407060	1.169614
6	-0.330040	1.407060	1.169614
7	-0.330040	1.407060	1.169614

This uses an average calculated from the first elements to estimate the missing values in the dataframe. If we apply the backfill method: print (dt.fillna(method='backfill')), it would return:

```
       1          2                   3
1  -2.289485  0.178246   0.894550
2  -0.724545  -0.531302  -1.720398
3   0.745967  0.954951   0.463451
4  -0.330040  1.407060   1.169614
5     NaN      NaN       NaN
6     NaN      NaN       NaN
7     NaN      NaN       NaN
```

The method shown here does not estimate, in this case, the missing values because it starts with the last elements in the dataframe to estimate missing values. In this case, all missing values are at the end of the dataframe, which yield to NaN values for the last elements of the dataframe.

We can delete the missing using the dropna() function as follows:

dt.dropna()

This function would return the following dataframe:

```
        1              2              3
1  -2.289485  0.178246   0.894550
2  -0.724545  -0.531302  -1.720398
3  0.745967   0.954951   0.463451
4  -0.330040  1.407060   1.169614
```

The pandas library allows merging and joining several dataframe objects using the merge() function. Let's create two dataframe objects.

```
import pandas as pd
male_list={'Name':
['Brian','Peter','Steve','Mark','Josh'],
            'Age': [100,20,30,40,50]
            }
female_list={ 'Name':
['Alice','Helen','Fallon','Silvia','Jane'],
            'Age':[10,20,30,40,50]
            }
dt1=pd.DataFrame(male_list)
dt2=pd.DataFrame(female_list)
```

Two dataframe objects we create are as below:

```
   Name Age
0 Brian 100
1 Peter 20
2 Steve 30
```

```
3 Mark 40
4 Josh 50
```

```
  Name  Age
0 Alice 10
1 Helen 20
2 Fallon 30
3 Silvia 40
4 Jane  50
```

Now let's merge the two dataframe objects according to a specific key. The key must found in both dataframe objects. For example, we can merge them by age:

>   dt=pd.merge(dt1,dt2,on='Age')

This function would merge according to the key passed as an argument to 'on' parameter. It creates a new dataframe object as follows:

```
  Name_x Age Name_y
0 Brian  10   Alice
1 Peter  20   Helen
2 Steve  30   Fallon
3 Mark   40   Silvia
4 Josh   50   Jane
```

We can notice that the resulted dataframe object is a combination of the two dataframe objects where they share the same age column. We can also merge dataframe objects according to several keys by passing a list of keys to 'on' argument of the merge() function.

The pandas library allows specifying how to merge the dataframe objects using the 'how' option. The 'how' option of the merge() function supports four options: left, right, inner, and outer. If the argument right is chosen, then the merging is applied using the key from the second dataframe object. If the left is specified, the merging is applied using keys from the first argument. If outer is specified for the merge() function, then it applies the union of keys. In contrast, if the inner is chosen, then it applies the intersection of keys to merge the dataframe objects.

To combine two dataframe objects in a single dataframe object, the concat() function can be used. The concat() function concatenates not only dataframe objects but also series objects. Let's for example concatenate the two dataframe objects of female and male in a single dataframe object:

```
import pandas as pd
male_list={'Name':
['Brian','Peter','Steve','Mark','Josh'],
```

```python
                    'Age': [10,20,30,40,50]
                }
    female_list={ 'Name':
['Alice','Helen','Fallon','Silvia','Jane'],
                    'Age':[10,20,30,40,50]
                }
    dt1=pd.DataFrame(male_list)
    dt2=pd.DataFrame(female_list)
    dt=pd.concat([dt1,dt2])
    print(dt)
```

The function returns:

```
  Name Age
0 Brian  10
1 Peter  20
2 Steve  30
3 Mark   40
4 Josh   50
0 Alice  10
1 Helen  20
2 Fallon 30
3 Silvia 40
4 Jane   50
```

We can set an indexing for the first and second dataframe objects in the concatenated dataframe object as follows:

```
dt=pd.concat([dt1,dt2],keys=['Male','Female'])
print(dt)
```

The output is as presented below:

```
         Name Age
Male   0 Brian 10
       1 Peter 20
       2 Steve 30
       3 Mark  40
       4 Josh  50
Female 0 Alice 10
       1 Helen 20
       2 Fallon 30
       3 Silvia 40
       4 Jane  50
```

Note in the resulted concatenated dataframe object in both examples presented above, the indexing is repeated. We can overcome this issue by setting ignore_index to True. This option allows ignoring the indexing in the dataframe objects passed to concat() function.

```
dt=pd.concat([dt1,dt2],keys=['Male','Female'],
ignore_index=True)
    print(dt)
```

The concat() function with ignore_index set to True returns:

```
  Name    Age
0 Brian   10
1 Peter   20
2 Steve   30
3 Mark    40
4 Josh    50
5 Alice   10
6 Helen   20
7 Fallon  30
8 Silvia  40
9 Jane    50
```

Note that when setting ignore_index to True, the keys are overridden too. In this case, the function used new indexing for the concatenated dataframe object.

We can use another built-in function that is also concatenating several dataframe objects of time series which append() function. Let's create three dataframe objects and apply the append() function to concatenate these dataframe objects.

    dt1=pd.DataFrame({'Name': ['Brian','Peter','Steve'], 'Age': [10,20,30]})

```
dt2=pd.DataFrame({ 'Name': ['Alice','Helen','Fallon'],
'Age':[10,20,30] })
dt3=pd.DataFrame({'Name':['Mark','Josh','Silvia'],
'Age':[20,30,50]})
dt=dt1.append([dt1,dt2,dt3])
print(dt)
```

The append function returns:

```
  Name   Age
0 Brian  10
1 Peter  20
2 Steve  30
0 Brian  10
1 Peter  20
2 Steve  30
0 Alice  10
1 Helen  20
2 Fallon 30
0 Mark   20
1 Josh   30
2 Silvia 50
```

The pandas library has two major functions to import the dataset into the workspace, namely read_csv() and read_table().

The first function read_csv() allows importing data from an excel file. The basic syntax for this function is:

pandas.read_csv(path_File)

We can also customize the different options this function offers by specifying the following options. The separating character and delimiter in the excel sheet, ignoring or not the header, names, index for the columns as well as names of the header and the how many rows to be ignored. The detailed syntax of the read_csv() function is as presented in the following statement:

pandas.read_csv(path_File, sep=';', delimiter=None, header='infer', names=None, index_col=None, usecols=None, skiprows=3)

We can also change the type of a variable in the imported table by using dtype as follows:

pandas.read_csv(filepath, dtype={'variable_name': np.float64})

The function read_table use the same syntax as read_csv to import tabular data as dataframe objects into Python workspace.

The library pandas allow handling dataframes as tables and performing SQL operations. It allows selecting, selecting with filters, group by. Let's create, for example, the following dataset and save it into an excel file name test.csv:

Name	Gender	Age	Smoker
Silvie	female	14	yes
Jean	male	19	yes
Joe	male	25	no
Brian	male	80	no
Helen	female	60	yes
Maxime	female	18	no

First, we should import the data as a dataframe object by naming the function read_csv():

```
import pandas as pd
data=pd.csv_read('test.xlsx')
```

The dataframe object should be similar to the output below:

	Name	Gender	Age	Smoker
0	Silvie	female	14	yes
1	Jean	male	19	yes
2	Joe	male	25	no
3	Brian	male	80	no
4	Helen	male	60	yes
5	Maxime	female	18	no

Now, let's explore how can we perform some of the SQL operations. To select a variable (column) from the table, we can simply specify the name of the variable between the bracket. For example, to get the age of all individual in the table, we type the following statement:

```
Age=data['Age']
print(Age)
```

The output is:

```
0  14
1  19
2  25
3  80
4  60
5  18
Name: Age, dtype: int64
```

We can also select several variables in one single statement by passing the list of the variables between the bracket. Let's say we want the age and whether the individual is a smoker or not. We can run the following statement:

```
Sub_data=data[['Age','Smoker']]
```

```
print(Sub_data)
```

The output is a table with the two variables 'Age' and 'Smoker':

```
  Age  Smoker
0  14  yes
1  19  yes
2  25  no
3  80  no
4  60  yes
5  18  no
```

We can apply a filter when selecting a variable. For example, let's select an individual with age over 20 years. We specify between brackets the condition on which the data should be selected as follows:

```
Sub_data=data[data['Age']>20]
print(Sub_data)
```

The function returns all variables for the individuals with age over 20 years as follows:

```
  Name  Gender  Age  Smoker
2  Joe   male    25  no
3  Brian male    80  no
4  Helen male    60  yes
```

We can also group data by specific characteristics using the groupby() function. For instance, we can group our data according to their gender as follows:

grouped_data=data.groupby('Gender')

After grouping them by their gender, we can get the number of individual for each group using the size() function:

print(grouped_data.size())

The output, in this case, is the number of female and male in the dataset:

```
Gender
female 2
male   4
dtype: int64
```

Overall, the pandas library is very handy to manipulate, explore, and analyze datasets. Now let's see the tools that we can use to make figures that help visualize and extract valuable information from datasets.

There are different tools in Python to create figures in Python. One forward library is a plot() library. Another advanced library with more options is the matplotlib library. These libraries allow plotting to scatter plots to detect correlation among variables. They allow creating figures of the histograms and distributions of data, which is very handy to make the first assumptions of the data distribution shape. Overall these libraries offer major features for data exploration analysis. We will use these libraries in the following chapter to develop machine learning applications. It is best to explore these libraries with real data. Therefore, we will not cover the details of these libraries in this chapter. You will learn the details of how to use these libraries in the next chapter with real data.

Another library that we will be using is the scikit-learn package. This package is an efficient Python tool for data analysis and machine learning. The scikit-learn library is based on the NumPy, SciPy and matplotlib libraries. It offers tools to perform data preprocessing, clustering, regression, model selection, classification, dimensionality reduction. It is free and open source library. This library offers several datasets in order to test machine learning algorithms. In the next chapter developing a machine learning model with Python, we will explore how to use this library to build, train, and evaluate machine learning models. All applications that we will be developing are based on the datasets available in this toolbox. Hence, we will not go through the options and functions of this toolbox in this chapter. We will rather go into the details of this library in the next chapter with examples using real data.

Chapter 4: Developing a Machine Learning Model With Python

In this chapter, we are going to apply the Python skills acquired in the previous chapter to develop machine learning models. We are going to use the Python libraries pandas for data processing, NumPy for numerical calculations and seaborn and matplotlib for visualization and finally the scikit-learn to use machine learning functions. We will be referring to the scikit-learn library as sklearn, which is the name used to import the library into Python workspace.

In example 1, we will go through a simple example of supervised learning with logistic regression for data classification. In this example, we will be using the Titanic dataset. We will build a model that predicts whether a titanic passenger would have survived or not according to several criteria. The Titanic dataset is available within the seaborn library.

In example 2, we will go through another method of supervised learning, which is linear regression. This example is based on the Boston housing dataset. We will develop a model that predicts house pricing using linear regression. The Boston housing is also available as a dataset in the sklearn library.

Example 3 and example 4 are applications to develop artificial neural networks. Both examples are using the same dataset, which is the Iris dataset. Example 3 is an initiation to develop a neural network by developing a simple perceptron. Example 4 is an application to develop a multi-layer neural network. You will learn through this example how to develop and train an artificial neural network from scratch. You will also learn how to develop the same model using built-in functions in Python.

All datasets used in the four examples are freely available online and are widely used as machine learning example applications.

In these examples, you will learn the necessary steps to develop a machine learning model for different applications.

Through these examples, you will not only learn how to develop machine learning models but also some new Python skills for data cleaning, plot, and visualize data. Basically, you will learn how to explore your data, how to check the presence of missing values, and how to convert your data into a data frame that is easily processed. You will also learn how to manage options of the plot functions to make readable figures.

Example 1: Logistic Regression

This application aims at developing a supervised machine learning model based on logistic regression. So, what are you going to learn in this example?

Through this example, you will learn the necessary steps to develop a logistic regression model with Python and how to use the built-in functions in Python libraries to build a logistic regression model. You will learn how to import data, how to visualize data and retrieve important information. You will also learn how to clean the dataset before building a machine learning classifier with logistic regression. We are also going cover how we can convert categorical variables into dummies variables which will be comprehensible by a regression model. Finally, we will go through how to create a training set from data, how to fit and evaluate the accuracy of the model. You will learn what a confusion matrix is, compute a confusion matrix, and how to analyze this matrix.

In this example, we are using the Titanic dataset that is widely used to illustrate a logistic regression model. Titanic dataset can be freely obtained from httpps://www.kaggle.com or can be loaded directly from the seaborn library. We all know the story of Titanic and the significant life loss that has been caused by the shipwreck due to the limited number of lifeboats. However, they were some passengers more likely to survive the sinking than others. These passengers that had luck play in their favor to survive the sinking were mainly children, women, and passenger of the upper class.

From the Titanic dataset, we are going to develop a predicting model that tells us whether a passenger on the Titanic would have survived or not based on different criteria.

First, we are going to load Python packages:

```
import pandas as pd
import numpy as np
import matplotlib.pyplot as plt
import seaborn as sns
```

Then, we import the titanic data coming from the seaborn library:

```
Titanic_data=sns.load_dataset('titanic')
```

Before starting the machine learning process, let's explore the dataset first. This step of data exploratory analysis is very important to understand how the data is stored and detect if there are any missing data or outliers.

With the following function, we are going to explore how the data is stored. It shows the first few lines of the data:

```
Titanic_data.head()
```

The output is as described in the following table. The first
column provides the passenger Id; the second column is a
binary variable (i.e., 0 or 1) that represents whether the
passenger had survived or not. The following columns provide
information about the passenger: pclass which is the ticket class
(1: upper, 2: middle and 3 is a lower class), sex, age, sibsp
number of siblings abroad, fare (i.e., passenger fare) and so on.
Note there is an additional variable alive that provides the same
information as a survived variable.

	survived	pclass	sex	age	sibsp	parch	fare	embarked	class	who	adult_male	deck	embark_town	alive	alone
0	0	3	male	22.0	1	0	7.2500	S	Third	man	True	NaN	Southampton	no	False
1	1	1	female	38.0	1	0	71.2833	C	First	woman	False	C	Cherbourg	yes	False
2	1	3	female	26.0	0	0	7.9250	S	Third	woman	False	NaN	Southampton	yes	True
3	1	1	female	35.0	1	0	53.1000	S	First	woman	False	C	Southampton	yes	False
4	0	3	male	35.0	0	0	8.0500	S	Third	man	True	NaN	Southampton	no	True

Sample of the Titanic dataset visualized with head() function.

Now let's see the size of the data. In other words, let's find how
many passengers are stored in this dataset. To do so, we use the
function:

Titanic_data.count()

The output of this function is:

```
survived        891
pclass          891
```

```
sex             891
age             714
sibsp           891
parch           891
fare            891
embarked        889
class           891
who             891
adult_male      891
deck            203
embark_town     889
alive           891
alone           891
dtype: int64
```

In total, 891 passengers, including the staff, were in the ship. We can see at this stage that there are some missing values for the variable age, deck, embarked, and embark_town. We will deal with this later. Now let's see how many people have survived in the Titanic. We are going to plot the number of people that had survived and had not survived as bars with countplot() function:

sns.countplot (x='survived', data=Titanic_data, palette=["k", "k"])

The countplot() function implemented in the seaborn library takes as input: x the variable for which we compute the frequency, data: the dataset. Palette is an option to specify the colors for each group, i.e., bar. In this example, both bars: survived and not survived are in black. The output of this function is given in the figure below. We note that more than 500 people did not survive the Titanic.

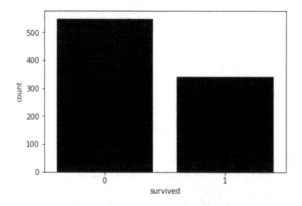

Bar plot of people that survived and did not survive the Titanic.

Now let's see the number of survivals according to the sex of passengers. To do so, we are going to add an option or a filter to the countplot() in order to specify that we want the counting of survivals for each sex separately. We are also going to change the colors. Because in this plot we will have four bars, we are going to create a palette color for our bar chart. This palette will be then passed as an argument for the countplot() function.

seq_palette=sns.color_palette('Greys',4)

```
sns.countplot (x='survived', hue='sex',
data=Titanic_data, palette=seq_palette)
```

The output should be similar to the figure below:

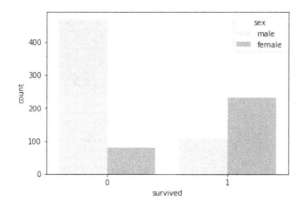

Survived passengers from the Titanic according to gender.

This figure shows us the more women have survived the Titanic than man. More than 400 men did not survive the Titanic, and only 100 mean approximately did survive the Titanic.

We can plot the same information according to the social class of passengers:

```
sns.countplot (x='survived', data=Titanic_data, hue='pclass',
palette=seq_palette)
```

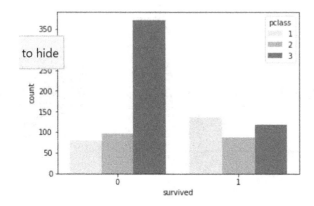

Survived passengers from the Titanic according to social class.

The figure shows the majority of people that did not survive the Titanic are from the lower class.

Now let's check the missing values in the dataset. To do so, we are going to compute the number of null values in the dataset:

Titanic_data.isnull().sum()

The function isnull() returns the variables with null values and sum() computes the sum. The output of the function given above is:

```
survived        0
pclass          0
sex             0
age           177
sibsp           0
parch           0
```

```
fare              0
embarked          2
class             0
who               0
adult_male        0
deck            688
embark_town       2
alive             0
alone             0
dtype: int64
```

We can notice the 177 values are missing for the variable age and 688 is missing for the deck variable and 2 missing values embark_town. There are several approaches to estimate missing values. These approaches are not covered in this book. We will rather focus on how to develop and train a prediction model. Therefore, these variables will not be used in the model and are going to be ignored. These variables will be dropped from the dataset with drop() function:

Titanic_data.drop('age',axis=1, inplace=True)

Titanic_data.drop('embark_town',axis=1, inplace=True)

Titanic_data.drop('deck',axis=1, inplace=True)

Titanic_data.dropna(inplace=True)

Titanic_data.head()

The axis option in the drop() function allows to specify if we want to drop column or row. Now the dataset is similar to this:

	survived	pclass	sex	sibsp	parch	fare	embarked	class	who	adult_male	alive	alone
0	0	3	male	1	0	7.25	S	Third	man	True	no	False
1	1	1	female	1	0	71.2833	C	First	woman	False	yes	False
2	1	3	female	0	0	7.925	S	Third	woman	False	yes	True
3	1	1	female	1	0	53.1	S	First	woman	False	yes	False
4	0	3	male	0	0	8.05	S	Third	man	True	no	True

Titanic dataset after deleting variables with missing values.

Now looking at the dataset above, we can see that 'who' variable, 'sex' variable and 'adult_male' provide the same information. The variable 'alive' is the same as the variable 'survived.' The variable 'class' and 'pclass also give the same information. Finally, we can retrieve the same information from the variable 'alone' and the variable 'sibsp.' Therefore, the variables 'who,' 'adult_male,' 'class,' 'alive' and 'alone' will be dropped from the dataset.

```
Titanic_data.drop(['class', 'who', 'adult_male', 'alive', 'alone'], axis=1,inplace=True)
```

The new Titanic dataset is like this:

	survived	pclass	sex	sibsp	parch	fare	embarked
0	0	3	male	1	0	7.25	S
1	1	1	female	1	0	71.283	C
2	1	3	female	0	0	7.925	S
3	1	1	female	1	0	53.1	S
4	0	3	male	0	0	8.05	S

The final dataset of Titanic.

Note that the variables 'sex' and 'embarked' are categorial. In order to make these variables easily processed by the machine learning algorithm, we need to transform these variables into dummies variables using the pandas library. Dummy variables are variables that take 0 or 1 value to indicate the presence of the category effect. In our example, we will create a dummy variable for 'sex' variable that is equal to 1 if gender is male and 0 otherwise. Another dummy variable that takes the value of 1 is embarked is S and 0 otherwise.

```
    sex=pd.get_dummies(Titanic_data['sex'],
drop_first=True)
    embarked=pd.get_dummies(Titanic_data['embarked'],
drop_first=True)
```

Then after, we drop the original 'sex' and 'embarked' variables and concatenate the new dummy variables into our Titanic dataset:

```
    Titanic_data.drop(['sex','embarked'],axis=1,inplace=True)
```

Titanic_data = pd.concat([Titanic_data, sex, embarked],axis=1)

Our final titanic dataset should like presented in the table below:

	survived	pclass	sibsp	parch	fare	male	Q	S
0	0	3	1	0	7.25	1	0	1
1	1	1	1	0	71.28	0	0	0
2	1	3	0	0	7.925	0	0	1
3	1	1	1	0	53.1	0	0	1
4	0	3	0	0	8.05	1	0	1

Now, our dataset is ready to create a logistic regression model. First, split our data into two datasets; the first that we will call the training dataset will be used to train the model. The second dataset will be called the test dataset will be used to assess the model's precision. To do so, we will employ the sklearn toolbox that we are going to import first. Then, we will apply the function train_test_split() to perform the splitting of the data.

In this example, the data features X we are using as predictors to predict if a passenger would have survived or not are: social class (pclass), number of siblings on board (sibsp), number of parents or children on board (parch), the fare, sex and embarked town. The labels Y to this dataset is the variable survived. When performing the data splitting with the train_test_split() we need to specify X, here is the Titanic dataset without the variable survived and the labels Y in this example is the survived variable. We also need to specify the percentage of the data that will be used as test data. Here, we will use 30% of the dataset to form the test data. The function is as follows:

```
X= Titanic_data.drop('survived',axis=1)
Y= Titanic_data['survived']
from sklearn.model_selection import train_test_split
Titanic_train, Titanic_test, Survived_train, Survived_test= train_test_split(X,Y, test_size=0.30,random_state=101)
```

Now we verify the size of our training and test datasets.

```
print('Size of the training dataset is ', Titanic_train.shape[0])
print('Size of labels of the training dataset is', Survived_train.shape[0])
print('Number of variables or features in the training dataset is ', Titanic_train.shape[1])
print(Size of the test data is ', Titanic_test.shape[0])
print('Size of labels of the test dataset is ', Survived_test.shape[0])
```

The output of this code is:

```
Size of the training dataset is 622
Size of labels of the training dataset is 622
Number of variables or features in the training dataset
is 7
Size of the test data is 267
Size of labels of the test dataset is 267
```

Now we have formed a training set which contains 70% of Titanic data. The test data is formed by 30% of the data as we have specified to train_test_split() function via the argument test_size.

Now let's build the logistic model. The sklearn library already has a built-in function to develop a logistic regression model which we are going to import:

> from sklearn.linear_model import LogisticRegression

After this, we will train the logistic regression model to the data:

> lnmodel = LogisticRegression()
> lnmodel.fit(Titanic_train,Surivived_train)

After fitting the model, we can use it to predict if passengers in the test dataset would have survived or not:

> Survival_Predictions = lnmodel.predict(Titanic_test)

The sklearn library also has a built-in function to evaluate the accuracy of the predictions made by the logistic regression model.

```
from sklearn.metrics import accuracy_score
print('Model accuracy is %2.3f', %
accuracy_score(Survived_test, Survival_Predictions))
```

This function returns:

Model accuracy is 0.824

The model is 82 % accurate, which means that the prediction made by the model is 82 % accurate. Now let's look at the confusion matrix. This matrix is very useful in appraising the machine learning classifier's efficiency as the one we developed for the Titanic data.

First, let's define what a confusion matrix is. The confusion matrix is a table providing a combination of predicted values and true values. In the example, we are working on we have predicted and true values of 0 and 1, i.e., survived or not survived. The confusion matrix will provide the frequency of estimated values as 1 when true values are equal to 1, frequency of estimated values of 1 whereas true values are equal to 0, frequency of estimated values of 0 whereas true values are 1 and frequency of estimated values of 0 when true values are also 0.

Basically, the confusion matrix describes the situations when the model predicts a "true positive" when the positive value predicted is the actual positive value. It also includes a prediction of a "false positive" if it's a positive value while actual value is negative, and it predicts negative value while actual value is positive. Finally, it is "true negative" when it predicts a negative value, and the actual value is negative (true negative). Theoretically, the table is as follows:

Confusion matrix

Predicted/True values	Positive (1)	Negative (0)
Positive (1)	(1|1) true positive	(1|0) false Positive
Negative (0)	(0|1) false negative	(0|0) true negative

Now let's look at the confusion table of our model.

```
from sklearn.metrics import confusion_matrix
confusion_matrix(Survived_test, Survival_Predictions)
```

The returned confusion matrix is:

```
array([[152, 11], [ 36, 68]], dtype=int64)
```

We can see that the number of times the model predicted false positive and false negative are very low compared to true positive and true negative, which reflects good accuracy and precision of the model.

Example 2: Linear Regression

This example aims at presenting an application of machine learning to develop a linear regression model. So, what will you learn through this example?

In this machine learning example, you will learn how to handle dictionary object in Python and how to get it features and keys. You will learn how to convert a dictionary object to a dataframe object in order to use pandas to analyze the data. You will learn how to plot data histogram and distribution as well as customizing the figure. You will learn to compute the summary statistics of the dataset. You will learn how to develop, fit, and evaluate the accuracy of a linear regression model.

In this example, the Boston housing pricing will be used. This data is available through the sklearn library. The Boston dataset is collected information about housing in Boston, MA. by U.S Census Service. This dataset was published first time in 1978 by Harrison and Rubinfel in the Journal of Environmental Economics and Management. Therefore, the data is not up to date is used for illustration purposes.

Like in example 1, we start first by importing the Python libraries and loading the dataset:

```
import numpy as np
import pandas as pd
#Visualization Libraries
import seaborn as sns
import matplotlib.pyplot as plt
from sklearn import datasets
boston_raw = datasets.load_boston()
```

If we check the type of this dataset with the type() function:

```
print(type(boston_raw))
```

The dataset is in the shape of a dictionary. We can get the dimensionality and the attributes of the dataset with the following commands:

```
print('Keys of the Boston dataset stored as dictionary
are:')
print(boston_raw.keys())
print('The dimension of the Boston dataset is')
print(boston_raw.data.shape)
print('The name of features in the Boston dataset are')
print(boston_raw.feature_names)
```

Now let's look at the output of this statement:

```
Keys of the Boston dataset stored as dictionary are:
dict_keys(['data', 'target', 'feature_names', 'DESCR',
'filename'])
The dimension of the Boston dataset is (506, 13)
The name of features in the Boston dataset are ['CRIM'
'ZN' 'INDUS' 'CHAS' 'NOX' 'RM' 'AGE' 'DIS' 'RAD' 'TAX'
'PTRATIO' 'B' 'LSTAT']
```

We have 506 observation and 13 variables where the name is the name of the features. Before going further in our data analysis, let's understand what each feature represents.

- CRIM: crime rate by town per capita
- ZN: the proportion of residential land zoned for lots over 25 000 sq.ft
- INDUS: the proportion of non-retail business acres per town
- CHAS: Charles River dummy variable (1 if tract bounds river, 0 otherwise)
- NOX: nitric oxides concentration (parts per 10 million)
- RM: average number of rooms per dwelling
- AGE: the proportion of owner-occupied units built prior to 1940
- DIS: weighted distances to five Boston employment centers

- RAD: index of accessibility to radial highways
- TAX: full-value property-tax rate per $10 000
- PTRATIO: pupil-teacher ratio by town
- B: $1000(Bk - 0.63)^2$ where Bk is the proportion of blacks by town
- LSTAT: % lower status of the population
- MEDV: Median value of the owner-occupied home in $1000's

You can get the description of the features presented above with the function:

    print(boston_raw.DESCR)

These features are the features that we will be used to predict the price of the house. Values of the housing are given by the 'target' key in the dataset. The dataset, as we have explored, is stored as a dictionary. We need to convert it to a data frame in order to be able to apply the pandas and numerical computation necessary to build our model. To do so, we run the following statements:

    boston_dt = pd.DataFrame(boston_raw.data, columns = boston_raw.feature_names)
    boston_dt['PRICE'] = boston_raw.target

The first statement converts the Boston housing dataset from a dictionary to a dataframe object. The second statement concatenate the created data frame and our target variable, which is the price. Now if we explore the first few lines of the dataset with the head() function, it looks like :

```
      CRIM    ZN  INDUS  CHAS    NOX     RM   AGE     DIS  RAD    TAX  \
0  0.00632  18.0   2.31   0.0  0.538  6.575  65.2  4.0900  1.0  296.0
1  0.02731   0.0   7.07   0.0  0.469  6.421  78.9  4.9671  2.0  242.0
2  0.02729   0.0   7.07   0.0  0.469  7.185  61.1  4.9671  2.0  242.0
3  0.03237   0.0   2.18   0.0  0.458  6.998  45.8  6.0622  3.0  222.0
4  0.06905   0.0   2.18   0.0  0.458  7.147  54.2  6.0622  3.0  222.0

   PTRATIO       B  LSTAT  PRICE
0     15.3  396.90   4.98   24.0
1     17.8  396.90   9.14   21.6
2     17.8  392.83   4.03   34.7
3     18.7  394.63   2.94   33.4
4     18.7  396.90   5.33   36.2
```

The Boston housing dataset.

Now we are going to do some exploratory analysis to better understand the data. We check first if there are any missing values:

```
boston_dt.isnull().sum()
```

Like in the first example, we computed the number of observations with missing values. This dataset does not contain any missing values:

```
CRIM      0
ZN        0
INDUS     0
```

```
CHAS          0
NOX           0
RM            0
AGE           0
DIS           0
RAD           0
TAX           0
PTRATIO       0
B             0
LSTAT         0
PRICE         0
dtype: int64
```

Now let's explore the range of house prices and their distribution. We are going to plot a histogram of the house prices to get a visual idea of the prices. We are going to use the seaborn library to plot the prices distribution and matplotlib library to control the figure features.

```
plt.figure(figsize=(5, 4)) # The figure size
sns.distplot(boston_dt['PRICE'], color='grey') # plot the
distribution and   histogram
plt.xlabel('price ($1000s)') # label of X-axis
plt.ylabel('Frequency') # label of Y-axis
plt.tight_layout()
plt.rc('xtick', labelsize=16) # Font size of the x-axis label
plt.rc('ytick', labelsize=16) # Font size of the y-axis label
```

plt.title('Histogram of House pricing', fontsize=18) # Title of the figure

The figure below provides the histogram and the distribution of the housing prices in Boston:

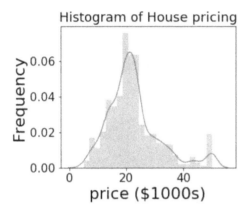

Distribution of the housing prices in Boston.

We can also plot the histogram with the matplotlib library with the following function.

```
hist(boston_dt['PRICE'])
```

This function, however, does not plot the curve of the distribution.

We can see from the figure above that price value are normally distributed with a median around 20 and values that range between 10 and 40 on a scale of $1000. We have some outliers with values around 50 in a $1000 scale.

Now let's explore the statistics of the features of the Boston housing prices dataset. We can get the basic statistics by the following function:

Boston_dt.describe()

This function returns a table with the main statistics for each feature as presented in the table below:

Summary Statistics of variables of the Boston housing dataset.

	CRIM	ZN	INDUS	CHAS	NOX	RM	AGE	DIS	RAD	TAX	PTRATIO	B	LSTAT	PRICE
count	506	506	506	506	506	506	506	506	506	506	506	506	506	506
mean	4	11	11	0	1	6	69	4	10	408	18	357	13	23
std	9	23	7	0	0	1	28	2	9	169	2	91	7	9
min	0	0	0	0	0	4	3	1	1	187	13	0	2	5
25%	0	0	5	0	0	6	45	2	4	279	17	375	7	17

50%	0	0	10	0	1	6	78	3	5	330	19	391	11	21
75%	4	13	18	0	1	7	94	5	24	666	20	396	17	25
max	89	100	28	1	1	9	100	12	24	711	22	397	38	50

The first row is the feature variable names. The second row is the number of observations for each feature variable. As we have already seen at the beginning of this example, we have 506 observations in this dataset. The third row is the average value for each feature. As described by the distribution function, the average value of prices is 23 in $1000's. The following statistic is the standard deviation. Some variables have high standard variation value like the variable 'B' which is a variable considering the proportion of blacks by the town. High values of standard deviation mean that the variable values are widespread. On the contrary, if the standard deviation is very low, it means that most of the values are around the average value. In other words, the high value of standard deviation means the variable ranges are wide, and low standard deviation means that the variable ranges are narrow and close to the average value.

We will try to forecast value of houses by developing a linear regression model. So, we are going to explore the correlated feature variables with respect to the price variable. We will plot the price variable versus each feature variable in a for loop:

```
feature_name=['ZN',
'INDUS','CHAS','NOX','RM','AGE','DIS','RAD','TAX','PTRATIO','B','LSTAT']
    fig = plt.figure(figsize=(10, 12))
    for i in range(0, len(feature_name)) :
        ax = fig.add_subplot(4, 3, i+1)
        plt.scatter(boston_dt[feature_name[i]],
    boston_dt['PRICE'],color='grey')
        plt.ylabel('Price', size=14,weight='bold')
        plt.xlabel(feature_name[i], size=14,weight='bold')
        plt.tight_layout()
```

The figure below shows the scatter plot of each feature variable and the price variable.

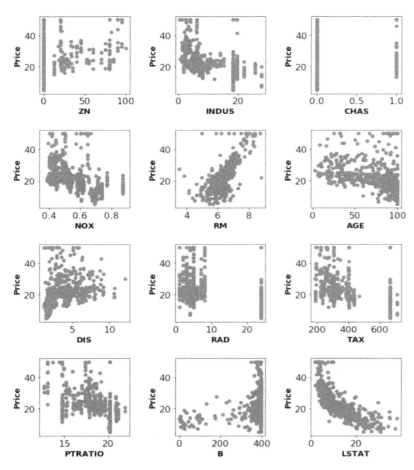

Scatter plot of the feature variables and the price variable of the Boston housing dataset.

We can see that some variables are highly correlated with the price like the 'RM' variable as the average quantity of chambers per dwelling and the 'LSTAT' variable as the percentage of the population's lower status. This variable is positively correlated with price. The price goes up when the number of rooms is increasing. The LSTAT is negatively correlated with the price. The price decrease when the % lower status of the population is increasing. We can also observe a moderate positive correlation between the price and the variable 'DIST,' the distance to five Boston employment centers. We can also notice that prices over 50 are not correlated with any variable. Let's confirm this statement by computing the correlation coefficient with the corrcoef() function of the Numpy library.

```
Selec_feature=['LSTAT','RM','DIS']
for i in range(0,len(Selec_feature)):
        print('Correlation coefficient between Price and ',
        Selec_feature[i], '=',
        np.corrcoef(boston_dt[Selec_feature[i]],boston_
        dt['PRICE'])[1][0])
```

The statements above returns:

Correlation coefficient between Price and LSTAT = -0.73766

Correlation coefficient between Price and RM = 0.6953599

Correlation coefficient between Price and DIS = 0.249928

As the variable LSTAT is the most correlated variable with the house prices, we are going to develop a linear regression model that predicts house prices based on this house feature. In other words, we build a model that explains or predict the house price according to the LSTAT:

```
X_boston=boston_dt['LSTAT']
Y_boston=boston_dt['PRICE']
```

We convert first our data into np.arrays:

```
X_boston=np.array(X_boston).reshape(-1,1)
Y_boston=np.array(Y_boston).reshape(-1,1)
```

Now, let's split the data onto two datasets. We will form a test set and training set as we did for the logistic regression example:

```
from sklearn.model_selection import train_test_split
boston_train, boston_test, price_train, price_test=
train_test_split(X_boston,Y_boston,
test_size=0.30,random_state=101)
```

We verify the size of all subset of data:

```
print('Size of X_train is', boston_train.shape)
print('Size of Y_train is', price_train.shape)
print('Size of X_test is',boston_test.shape)
print('Size of y_test is',price_test.shape)
```

The output of these statements is

```
Size of X_train is (354, 1)
Size of Y_train is (354, 1)
Size of X_test is (152, 1)
Size of y_test is (152, 1)
```

The training set is 354 in size, and the size of the test set is 152. Now we import from the sklearn library the module linear regression and fit the model:

```
from sklearn.linear_model import LinearRegression
LnReg = LinearRegression()
        LnReg.fit(boston_train, price_train)
```

After running the statements above, fit function returns:

```
LinearRegression(copy_X=True,
fit_intercept=True, n_jobs=None,
normalize=False)
```

To evaluate model performance, the fitted model is applied to estimate house prices with the feature LSTAT in the test dataset boston_test:

```
y_estimated=LnReg.predict(boston_test)
```

Then, we compute the coefficient of determination R^2 and the Root Mean Square Error of the estimated data. The RMSE should be close to 0 and R^2 should be close to 1.

```
from sklearn.metrics import mean_squared_error
RMSE=(np.sqrt(mean_squared_error(y_test,
y_estimated)))
R2=round(LnReg.score(X_test, y_test),2)
```

The RMSE of this model is 6.95, and the R² is 0.51.

Now let's develop a multi-variable linear model and compare it with a single variable that we have developed. We follow the same steps. We don't need to import all the libraries because they are already imported.

```
Y=boston_dt
X=boston_dt.drop('PRICE',axis=1)
X_train, X_test, y_train, y_test= train_test_split(X,Y,
test_size=0.30,random_state=101)
LnReg1 = LinearRegression()
LnReg1.fit(X_train, y_train)
```

We evaluate the model performance to forecast the prices of the training dataset:

```
y_train_estimated = LnReg1 .predict(X_train)
RMSE = (np.sqrt(mean_squared_error(y_train,
y_train_estimated)))
R2 = round(LnReg1.score(X_train, y_train),2)
print('RMSE for the training dataset is: ', RMSE)
print('R2 for the training dataset is: ', R2)
```

The RMSE for the training dataset is 1.17 and R2 is 1, which is expected because this dataset was used for training the model.

Now we evaluate the model performance to predict the house prices for the test data set.

```
y_test_estimated = LnReg1 .predict(X_test)
RMSE = (np.sqrt(mean_squared_error(y_test,
y_test_estimated)))
R2 = round(LnReg1.score(X_test, y_test),2)
print('RMSE for the test dataset is: ', RMSE)
print('R2 for the test dataset is: ', R2)
```

The RSME for the test dataset is 1.42 and R2 is almost 1. We can see by including more features in the model we increased the accuracy of the model. The scatter plot of the actual prices versus the estimated price confirm the accuracy of the model.

```
fig = plt.figure(figsize=(5, 4))
plt.scatter(y_test, y_test_estimated,color='grey')
plt.ylabel('Estimated price ($1000)',
size=14,weight='bold')
plt.xlabel('True price ($1000)', size=14,weight='bold')
plt.tight_layout()
```

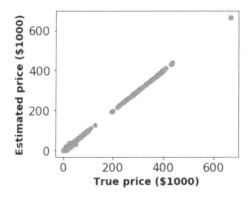

Scatter plot of predicted prices and the actual prices.

Example 3: Perceptron

The current example is an initiation to develop a neural network with Python. We will develop a perceptron, a single layer neural network, to classify the Iris data. You will learn in this example how to explore the dataset and create figures. You will learn how to develop, train, and evaluate the accuracy of a perceptron using the built-in functions of Python.

The Iris data used in this example as well as in the following example is a multivariate dataset widely used in machine learning. It is used as an application illustration of building a classifier. The Iris dataset is composed of several samples of 3 species of the Iris flower. Features that are available to discriminate between the species are both sepals and petals length and sepals and petals width. According to the combination of these features, we are going to build a model with a perceptron to discriminate between the species. This dataset is freely available within the sklearn library.

First, we import Python libraries and load the data from the sklearn library:

```
import numpy as np
import pandas as pd
#Visualization Libraries
import seaborn as sns
import matplotlib.pyplot as plt
from sklearn import datasets
Iris = datasets.load_iris()
```

First, we check the type of the data:

```
print(type(Iris))
```

The function returns:

```
<class 'sklearn.utils.Bunch'>
```

We can see that data is stored as a dictionary. Now we inspect the sizes of the different features of the dataset:

```
print('Keys of the Iris dataset stored as dictionary are:')
print(Iris.keys())
print('The dimension of the Iris dataset is')
print(Iris.data.shape)
print('The name of features in the Iris dataset are')
print(Iris.feature_names)
```

The statements above return:

```
Keys of the Iris dataset stored as
dictionary are: dict_keys(['data',
'target', 'target_names', 'DESCR',
'feature_names', 'filename'])
The dimension of the Iris dataset is (150,
4)
The name of features in the Iris dataset
are ['sepal length (cm)', 'sepal width
(cm)', 'petal length (cm)', 'petal width
(cm)']
```

The four variables or features of the Iris flower are stored as follows:

sepal length (cm)	sepal width (cm)	petal length (cm)	petal width (cm)	Species
5.1	3.5	1.4	0.2	0
4.9	3	1.4	0.2	0
4.7	3.2	1.3	0.2	0
4.6	3.1	1.5	0.2	0
5	3.6	1.4	0.2	0

In total, we have 150 data of Iris flower. The four features, such as the petal width and length and sepal width and length, are measured in centimeter. We have 50 samples of each species. The species (i.e., target variable) are already in the form of dummy variable with values of 0, 1,2 where each index is associated with a specific specie. Iris setosa is indexed with 0; Iris verginica is indexed as 1 and Iris versicolor is indexed as 2. Now let's get the summary statistics of each species using the following:

Iris.data.describe()

The summary statistics are:

	sepal length (cm)	sepal width (cm)	petal length (cm)	petal width (cm)
count	150	150	150	150
mean	5.843	3.057	3.758	1.199
std	0.828	0.436	1.765	0.762

min	4.3	2	1	0.1
25%	5.1	2.8	1.6	0.3
50%	5.8	3	4.35	1.3
75%	6.4	3.3	5.1	1.8
max	7.9	4.4	6.9	2.5

We retrieve the feature data and the target variable:

```
X_Iris=Iris.data
Y_Iris=Iris.target
```

Let's explore properties of each Iris species:

```
plt.scatter(X_Iris[np.where(Y_Iris==0),0],X_Iris[np.where(Y_Iris==0),1],color='k',marker='o',label='setosa')
plt.scatter(X_Iris[np.where(Y_Iris==1),0],X_Iris[np.where(Y_Iris==1),1],color='k',marker='*',label='versicolor')
plt.scatter(X_Iris[np.where(Y_Iris==2),0],X_Iris[np.where(Y_Iris==2),1],color='k',marker='+',label='verginica')
plt.xlabel('petal length (cm)')
plt.ylabel('sepal length(cm)')
plt.legend(loc='best')
plt.show()
```

The figure below presents the sepal length versus the petal length for three Iris species setosa, versicolor, and verginica. We can already distinguish setosa species from the other two species according to the sepal and petal length.

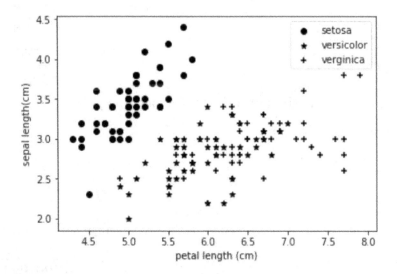

Scatter plot of the sepal and petal length of the Iris species.

From the scatter above of the three species we can see that there is no difference between versicolor and verginica species. So, we merge these two species into one single class as follows:

```
Y_Iris= (Iris.target==0).astype(np.int8)
print(Y_Iris)
```

We simply assigned the index 1 to the setosa Iris and 0 to the others. The target variable now is:

```
[1 1 1 1 1 1 1 1 1 1 1 1 1 1 1 1 1 1 1 1 1 1 1
 1 1 1 1 1 1 1 1 1 1 1 1 1 1 1 1 1 1 1 1 1 1 1
 1 1 1 0 0 0 0 0 0 0 0 0 0 0 0 0 0 0 0 0 0 0 0 0
 0 0 0 0 0 0 0 0 0 0 0 0 0 0 0 0 0 0 0 0 0 0 0 0
```

```
0 0 0 0 0 0 0 0 0 0 0 0 0 0 0 0 0 0 0 0 0 0 0 0 0 0
0 0 0 0 0 0 0 0 0 0 0 0 0 0 0 0 0 0 0 0 0 0 0 0 0 0
0 0 0 0 0 0 0]
```

We divide the data onto 2 datasets one will be used for training the model, and the second for assessing the accuracy of the model:

```
from sklearn.model_selection import train_test_split
Iris_train, Iris_test, Species_train, Species_test = train_test_split(X_Iris, Y_Iris, test_size=0.3)
```

In this example, we are going to use the sklearn library to build the perceptron:

```
from sklearn.linear_model import Perceptron
```

We make a perceptron object with a learning rate of 0.1 and a maximum iteration of 100:

```
Perc_model = Perceptron(max_iter=100, tol=0.19,eta0=0.1, random_state=0)
```

Then we fit the perceptron with the Iris_train dataset:

```
Perc_model.fit(Iris_train, Species_train)
```

The training statement returns:

```
Perceptron(alpha=0.0001, class_weight=None,
early_stopping=False, eta0=0.1,
fit_intercept=True, max_iter=100, n_iter=None,
n_iter_no_change=5, n_jobs=None, penalty=None,
random_state=0, shuffle=True, tol=0.19,
validation_fraction=0.1, verbose=0,
warm_start=False)
```

The perceptron object has as attribute the coefficient (W), intercept (b), and a number of iterations to achieve convergence criteria. We can access these by calling the Perceptron object with the attributes:

```
print('Perceptron weights: ', Perc_model.coef_)
print('Perceptron bias:', Perc_model.intercept_)
print('Number of itr to stop criteria:',
Perc_model.n_iter_)
```

The attributes of the Perceptron developed in this example are:

```
Perceptron weights: [[ 0.09 0.44 -0.67 -0.3] [
1.51 -2.16 1.28 -2.07] [-2.66 -1.72 3.33 3.35]]
Perceptron bias: [ 0.1 0.7 -1.1]
Number of itr to stop criteria: 8
```

Now we evaluate the performance of the perceptron to classify the Iris species of the test dataset.

```
y_estimated = Perc_model.predict(X_test)
from sklearn.metrics import accuracy_score
print('Accuracy of the model : %.2f' %
accuracy_score(y_test, y_estimated))
```

The accuracy of the perceptron is 0.98. This means that the model classifies 98% of the data accurately.

Example 4: Multi-Layer Neural Network

The aim of this example is to guide you through the steps to develop a multi-layer neural network. In this application, you will learn how to develop an artificial neural network from scratch. In other words, we will not use any library to develop or train the artificial neural network. Instead, we will develop several functions that will serve to model each component of the neural network. We will develop functions that simulate the functioning of the artificial neural network and the algorithm gradient descent to fit the neural network. We will be developing all the necessary functions that compute the component of a neural network: weights, cost function, forward propagation, and back propagation and finally, the function that updates the weights. We will use the same dataset as the previous example, the Iris dataset.

Finally, in this example, we will present how we can develop and train an artificial neural network using the built-in functions in Python. You will acquire knowledge of how to select a specific optimization algorithm to train the neural network, activation function, size of hidden layers as well as the parameter that sets the learning rate. To train the multi-layer neural network and compare their accuracy, we will employ two different algorithms.

First, we have to load our packages and the data from the sklearn library:

```
import pandas as pd
from sklearn import datasets
Iris = datasets.load_iris()
X=Iris.data
```

We have noticed in the previous example, developing a Perceptron as a classifier for the Iris data, that the Iris versicolor and verginica are very similar and cannot be distinguished. We merge these two species as a single class as we did by assigning an index 1 if it is 1 to setosa Iris follower and 0 otherwise:

```
Y= (Iris.target==0).astype(np.int8)
```

To develop the multi-layer neural network from scratch, we are going first to write a function that returns the size of the dataset:

```
def Get_sizes(X, Y):
    s_x = X.shape[0] # Input layer size
```

```
s_h = 7# hidden layers size
s_y = Y.shape[0] # Output layer size
return (s_x, s_h, s_y)
```

We are going next to write a function that initialize the neural network parameters:

```
def Init(s_X, s_h, s_Y):
    W1 = np.random.randn(s_h, s_X) * 0.01 #weight
matrix of shape (s_h, s_x)
    b1 = np.zeros(shape=(s_h, 1)) #bias vector of shape (s_h, 1)
    W2 = np.random.randn(s_Y, s_h) * 0.01  #weight matrix
of shape (s_y, s_h)
    b2 = np.zeros(shape=(s_Y, 1)) #bias vector of shape (s_y, 1)
    Param = {"W1": W1,
             "b1": b1,
             "W2": W2,
             "b2": b2}
    return Param
```

The above procedure returns an initial weights matrices and vectors W1, W2, b1, and b2 according to the size of the input and output layers.

Next, we define the activation functions we will use in the multi-layer network, namely the sigmoid and ReLu functions.

```
def Sigmoid(Z):
    return 1/(1+np.exp(-Z))


def Relu(Z):
    return np.maximum(0,Z)
```

Now, we are going to define a function that performs the forward propagation in the neural network. This function basically multiplies input data X by the weights of the first layer W1 and add the bias matrix b1. Then, it applies the ReLu activation that provides the output of the first layer A1. Next, it multiplies A1 by the weight matrix of the second layer W2 and adds the bias matrix b2. The Sigmoid activation is then applied to the output A2, which is the output of the network. This function returns outputs of each layer as well as the values of the activation functions.

```
def fd_Propagation(Z,Param):
    Z1 = np.dot(Param['W1'],Z)+Param['b1']
    A1 = Relu(Z1)
    Z2=np.dot(Param['W2'],A1)+Param['b2']
    A2 = Sigmoid(Z2)
    ch={'Z1': Z1,
```

```
        'A1': A1,
        'Z2': Z2,
        'A2': A2
    }
    return ch
```

After the forward propagation, we need to evaluate the accuracy of the estimated output. To do so, we write a function that compute the cost function.

```
def cost_fct(A2,Y):
    m = len(Y)
    tmp = np.multiply(np.log(A2), Y) + np.multiply((1 - Y), np.log(1 - A2))
    cost = - np.sum(tmp) / m
    return cost
```

The function defined above cost_fct() returns the neural network error. The function takes the estimated output and the target value as inputs.

In order to fit the multi-layer network, we need to develop a gradient algorithm that will optimize the artificial neural network. In other words, we must estimate the best weight combination which minimizes the cost function. To do so, we need to compute the gradient for the activation functions. For that, we write the two functions that provide the gradient for the Sigmoid and Relu functions:

```
def dRelu(Z):
        Z[Z<=0] = 0
        Z[Z>0] = 1
        return Z


def dSigmoid(Z):
  c = 1/(1+np.exp(-Z))
  dZ = c * (1-c)
  return dZ
```

We also need to compute the gradient for the weight's matrices. This process is called the backward propagation. We write the following function that we called bd_Propagation:

```
def bd_Propagation(Param,ch,E,F,):
        m=E.shape[1]
        W1=Param['W1']
        W2=Param['W2']
        A1=ch['A1']
        A2=ch['A2']
        dF = - (np.divide(F,A2 ) - np.divide(1 -F, 1-A2))
        dZ2 = dLoss_Yh * dSigmoid(Z2)
        dA1 = np.dot(W2.T,dZ2)
```

```
        dW2 = 1./A1.shape[1] * np.dot(dZ2,A1.T)
        db2 = 1./A1.shape[1] * np.dot(dZ2,
np.ones([dZ2.shape[1],1]))
    dZ1 = dA1 * dRelu(Z1)
        dA0 = np.dot(W1,dZ1)
        dW1 = 1./E.shape[1] * np.dot(dZ1,F)
        db1 = 1./E.shape[1] * np.dot(dZ1,
np.ones([dZ1.shape[1],1]))
        gradients={
                'dW1': dW1,
                'db1': db1,
                'dW2': dW2,
                'db2': db2
        }
        return gradients
```

This function takes as input the weights and the output of the forward propagation function (i.e. fd_Propagation) and the input and output layers to compute the gradients. Then, we write the function Update() that updates the gradients :

```
    def Update(Param, gradients, alpha):
        W1=Param['W1']-alpha*gradients['dW1']
        W2=Param['W2']-alpha*gradients['dW2']
        b1=Param['b1']-alpha*gradients['db1']
        b2=Param['b2']-alpha*gradients['db2']
```

```
        Param = {"W1": W1,
            "b1": b1,
      "W2": W2,
      "b2": b2}
        return Param
```

The Update() function updates the weights matrices by subtracting the product of the learning rate and the gradients for each weight matrix. The learning rate (called alpha) is a parameter that controls the speed by which the networks learn. The weights are updated by a proportion controlled by the learning rate. Now that we have developed all the functions necessary for the forward propagation, the cost function and back propagation, let's assemble the algorithm the Gradient descent algorithm in order to fit the neural network. The gradient descent algorithm will perform in serial the following tasks: initialization of the parameters, perform the forward propagation, compute the cost function, perform back propagation to compute the gradients, update the parameters and repeat the process from the forward propagation until it attains the maximum number of iterations. The procedure is as follows:

```
    def Gradient_descent(X, Y, nbr_itr=500,
print_cost_fct=False):
            np.random.seed()
```

```
        s_X, s_h, s_Y=Get_sizes(X,Y)
        Param = Init(s_X, s_h, s_Y)
        for k in range(0, nbr_itr):
                ch = fd_Propagation(X, Param)
                A2=ch['A2']
                cost = cost_fct(A2, Y, Param)
                gradients = backward_propagation(Param,
ch, X, Y)

                Param = Update(Param, gradients)
                if print_cost_fct and k % 500 == 0:
                        print ("Cost after iteration %k: %f" %
                        (k, cost))
        return Param, s_h
```

Now we can run the model with the Iris dataset:

```
    Gradient_descent(X, Y, nbr_itr=500,
print_cost_fct=False)
```

Instead of developing a multi-layer neural network from scratch, library sklearn can be used.

```
        import pandas as pd
        from sklearn import datasets
        Iris = datasets.load_iris()
        X=Iris.data
```

The Iris versicolor and verginica are very similar and cannot be distinguished. We merge these two species as a single class as we did before by assigning an index 1 if it is 1 to steosa Iris follower and 0 otherwise:

> Y= (Iris.target==0).astype(np.int8)

We divide the data onto 2 sets for fitting and evaluation of the accuracy of the neural network:

> from sklearn.model_selection import train_test_split
> Iris_train, Iris_test, Species_train, Species_test = train_test_split(X, Y, test_size = 0.30)

We create a neural network as a multi-layer classifier using the function MLPCLassifier (). We specify the size of hidden layers, i.e., a number of nodes of each layer, how many hidden layers in the network as well as the number of maximum iterations for the gradient descent algorithm:

> from sklearn.neural_network import MLPClassifier
> ANN = MLPClassifier(hidden_layer_sizes=(10, 10, 10), max_iter=1000)

Here we created multi-layer classifier with 10 hidden layers and maximum iteration number of 1000.

We can then train the artificial neural network and make predictions:

ANN.fit(Iris_train, Species_train)

The training function returns :

```
MLPClassifier(activation='relu', alpha=0.0001,
batch_size='auto', beta_1=0.9, beta_2=0.999,
early_stopping=False, epsilon=1e-08,
hidden_layer_sizes=(10, 10, 10),
learning_rate='constant',
learning_rate_init=0.001, max_iter=1000,
momentum=0.9, n_iter_no_change=10,
nesterovs_momentum=True, power_t=0.5,
random_state=None, shuffle=True, solver='adam',
tol=0.0001, validation_fraction=0.1,
verbose=False, warm_start=False)
```

We can see from the output of the fit function that by default, the activation function used in the neural network we developed is the ReLu function with the learning rate parameter of 0.0001 (i.e., alpha parameter). The optimizer used by default is 'adam.' The adam algorithm is a new optimization algorithm developed for training neural networks. This procedure adjusts the learning rate during optimization. We can change the solver algorithm when we create the multi-layer classifier as follows:

ANN_sgd =
MLPClassifier(hidden_layer_sizes=10,solver='sgd',learning_rat
e_init= 0.01, max_iter=500)

Here, we created the multi-layer classifier object with the stochastic gradient descent(sgd) algorithm and learning rate equal to 0.01.

Fitting this multi-layer neural network:

ANN_sgd.fit(Iris_train, Species_train)

returns :

```
MLPClassifier(activation='relu', alpha=0.0001,
batch_size='auto', beta_1=0.9,
    beta_2=0.999, early_stopping=False, epsilon=1e-08,
    hidden_layer_sizes=10, learning_rate='constant',
    learning_rate_init=0.01, max_iter=500, momentum=0.9,
    n_iter_no_change=10, nesterovs_momentum=True,
power_t=0.5,
    random_state=None, shuffle=True, solver='sgd',
tol=0.0001,
    validation_fraction=0.1, verbose=False,
warm_start=False)
```

Now let's predict the Iris flower species in the test dataset using both multi-layer neural network fitted with adam and stochastic gradient descent algorithms

Y_adam = ANN.predict(Iris_test)
Y_sgd=ANN_sgd.predict(Iris_test)

The predicted output with both classifiers:

```
        print('Predicted species with adam algo:', Y_adam)
        print('Predicted species with sgd algo:', Y_sgd)
```

is:

```
Predicted species with adam algo: [1 1 0 0 0 0 0 0 0 1 1
0 0 0 1 1 0 0 0 0 0 0 0 1 0 1 0 0 0 1 1 0 1 0 0 0 0
 0 0 1 0 1 0 1 1]
Predicted species with sgd algo: [1 1 0 0 0 0 0 0 0 1 1 0
0 0 1 1 0 0 0 0 0 0 0 1 0 1 0 0 0 1 1 0 1 0 0 0 0
 0 0 1 0 1 0 1 1]
```

Finally, we evaluate the accuracy of the artificial neural network trained with adam optimization algorithm using the confusion matric that we defined in the example 2 and the accuracy score:

```
        from sklearn.metrics import confusion_matrix
        print('Confusion matrix is':
confusion_matrix(Species_test, Y_adam))
        from sklearn.metrics import accuracy_score
        print('Accuracy of the model: %.2f %
accuracy_score(Species_test, Y_adam))
```

After running these statements, they return:

```
Confusion matrix is [[30 0] [ 0 15]]
Accuracy of the model: 1.00
```

Now let's compare this confusion matrix with confusion matrix of the model optimized with adam algorithm and evaluate how accurate the artificial neural network is with the stochastic gradient descent algorithm:

```
from sklearn.metrics import confusion_matrix
print('Confusion matrix is': mconfusion_matrix(y_test,
Y_sgd))
from sklearn.metrics import accuracy_score
print('Accuracy of the model: %.2f %
accuracy_score(y_test, Y_sgd))
```

Running these statements provide the following output:

```
Confusion matrix is [[30 0] [ 0 15]]
Accuracy of the model: 1.00
```

We note here that results are similar regardless of the solver or the optimization algorithm used. The model is 100% accurate. We obtained similar accuracy with the perceptron in the previous example. The accuracy obtained in these examples is good to given the small size of the dataset (i.e., only 150 of Iris samples). This example raises the issue around overfitting artificial neural networks. We used 70% of the dataset to train the model and 30% to test the ability of the model to make a good prediction. Let's change the size of the training and test datasets and see if it would affect the model accuracy. For example, we divide the Iris data in half:

```
from sklearn.model_selection import train_test_split
```

Iris_train, Iris_test, Species_train, Species_test = train_test_split(X, Y, test_size = 0.50)

Then we follow the same steps. Because Adam algorithm and the stochastic gradient algorithm yield to similar results, we will create a neural network that is multi-layer using stochastic gradient descent algorithm as a solver for training the model:
ANN_sgd = MLPClassifier(hidden_layer_sizes=10,solver='sgd',learning_rate_init= 0.01, max_iter=500)

Now, we train and predict using the new model:
```
ANN_sgd.fit(Iris_train, Species_train)
Y_sgd=ANN_sgd.predict(Iris_test)
```
Finally, we evaluate the confusion matrix and the model accuracy:
```
from sklearn.metrics import confusion_matrix
print('Confusion matrix is':
mconfusion_matrix(Species_test, Y_sgd))
from sklearn.metrics import accuracy_score
print('Accuracy of the model: %.2f' %
accuracy_score(Species_test, Y_sgd))
```

The statements above return:
```
Confusion matrix is [[47 0] [ 0 28]]
```

```
Accuracy of the model: 1.00
```

The new trained neural network on half of the data has similar accuracy and precision of the neural network trained on 70% of data.

Conclusion

Thank you for making it to the end of *Machine Learning With Python.* Let us hope that it was informative and able to provide you with all of the tools you need to achieve your goals whatever they may be.

The objective of this book is to present an introduction for the absolute beginners to machine learning and data science. The book presents the reasoning behind machine learning and its methods as well as a guide for using Python to apply those methods.

This book covers the major machine learning paradigms, namely supervised, unsupervised, semi-supervised, and reinforcement. The book also covers artificial neural network principles in a separate chapter. This book explains how to develop machine learning models in general and how to develop a neural network which is a particular method of performing machine learning. It teaches how to train and evaluate their accuracy.

Python is a widely used programming language for different applications and in particular for machine learning. This book covers the basic Python programming as well as a guide to use Python libraries for machine learning.

This book presents machine learning applications using real datasets to help you enhance your Python programming skills as well as machine learning basics acquired through the book. These applications provide examples of developing a machine learning model for predictions using linear regression, a classifier using logistic regression and artificial neural network. Through these applications, examples of data exploration and visualization using Python are presented.

Machine learning is an active research subject, in particular, artificial neural networks. Nowadays, machine learning is used in every domain, such as marketing, health care systems, banking systems, stock market, gaming applications, among others. This book's objective is to provide a basic understanding of the major branches of machine learning as well as the philosophy behind artificial neural networks. The book also aims at providing Python programming skills for machine learning to beginners with no previous programming skills in Python or any other programming language.

Once you have acquired the skills and understood the reasoning behind machine learning models presented in this book, you will be able to use these skills to solve complex problems using machine learning. You will also be able to easily acquire other skills and use more advanced machine learning methods.

Finally, if you found this book useful in any way, a review on Amazon is always appreciated!

CPSIA information can be obtained
at www.ICGtesting.com
Printed in the USA
LVHW052044310121
677957LV00035B/1816

9 781914 306136